G....

Love letters on loss, grief, and self

Liz Lethbridge

Dying was the end of a long beginning.

ISBN: 9798405195155
Independently Published, 2022

Editor's Preface

I think it would be a good idea to say a little about my mother and indicate something of the rich stories that she and we her family have been part of over getting on for seven decades.

My grandmother we boys loved dearly. We called her 'Granny', but her name was 'Daisy Bell' and we called her this, too. Short, plump, Colchester English, sweet and easily hurt by carelessness or the feeling that she was not needed. Her warm east-Essex vowels were beautiful; she told us stories real and imagined. My grandfather I saw only a few times when we went down to Colchester to visit. He had been a soldier (of the Kipling variety I fancy) and lost first one and then the other eye in the Great War. He was said to have fought in both wars, but we can't find records to that effect. I was fascinated by him, and more because blood is thick than because I saw him often (I didn't), I loved him, too. His chin was prickly under the obligatory hallo and goodbye kisses, his tobacco smelt strongly (I loved that, too), and I couldn't understand much of what he said for his dialect was strong. He wore his flat cap in the house, he sat by the coal fire which was kept alight all year round as was the way in those days. He didn't like to be helped in moving around the tiny house, but when I knew him he was already a wee bit frail and sometimes had to endure the leading hand of a tiny boy. He died when I was six and Granny's visits became longer, to our delight.

Editor's Preface

Granny told us that she never had to discipline my mother. My mother told a different story, but only for the record's sake. My mother's childhood was obviously difficult, it did include foster parents, but she wouldn't talk about it, not to we boys, nor to my father. She would talk a bit about the war, dogfights overhead, the front door climbing the stairs during one bombing raid, stories of being in service in a posh house when my father was courting her. That was it. The first chapter was over when she met my father. Raising three boys, born just inside three years, on the very small salary my father earned (this never really changed), determination that we should have the childhood she didn't, was the next chapter, and a happy one it was. Discipline was strict and my mother had a formidable personality and not a little temper; but the warm love was stronger and she had also a loving, fair and generous personality, as protective as an over-anxious mother hen, but never restrictive or suffocating.

The Great Event in all our lives was the six years spent in West Africa where my Father worked for the church, first as business manager, then general secretary, and eventually as a pastor; but also as builder, plumber, mechanic and what not?, as was the way in those days. We arrived in Nigeria just after the Biafran War had broken out, and left just after it had come to an end. We children had our own experience of war. These were the happiest days of our lives. We didn't live in the posh area of Ibadan, but on the mission compound close to the old heart of the great city, though we went to the International School on the other side of town. Once school was finished for the day or the week and during the holidays we boys played on the compound and in the densely populated, rather poor area around it, with the other local children. As our friends learnt or improved their English from us, so we learnt Yoruba and Nigerian ways from them. We were immensely fortunate in this, many of these friends still remain, and they came in force to my father's funeral, turning it in a way he would have approved, which in fact he had asked for, from an occasion of mourning to an occasion of celebration and joy, to the immense comfort of my mother, we boys and Elizabeth and many of a large extended family. By the time we left Ibadan, apart from the colour of our skins we could have passed off as Nigerian boys ourselves. In Liberia, we lived deep in the bush on a large school campus. My mother informally adopted the roles of nurse, matron and general port of first call, as well as that of a pastor's wife, often called upon for large scale entertainment when my father's superiors came to visit, largely from the USA, Scandinavia and the UK. She excelled in all these roles, as, despite her modesty and lack of confidence she has -- by native genius, instinct and a strength of personality that can carry all before it, though never trampling over other people -- excelled in all that she has put her hand to, or has had to put her hand to. She took no nonsense from anyone, but was always fair. She and my father were much loved in West Africa, at root, I think this was because first of a genuine interest in other people which was neither pretended, nor forced, nor cultivated; second because they respected other people. This was often commented on in the only apparently trivial observation that my parents always said, and meant it, please and thank you. My mother could issue orders well enough, in that manner that brooked no dissent and as a result got none, but that was only in extremis; there is also an art to saying please such that the request is only an order in disguise, and my mother was past mistress of that, too, if occasion warranted it. Usually it was just good manners to whomever you were speaking to, great or small young or old, to say please and then thank you. And above all to apologise if that were necessary. None of this happens genuinely unless you see people as people and are interested in them. But that doesn't necessarily mean that you like every one, nor that you are sweetness and light all the time. Mummy certainly wasn't. For one thing, she had too lively a sense of humour, and saw the ridiculous in a great many affectations and insincerities, and was just as likely to laugh irreverently with you (never at you, it is not in her nature) and bring you to laugh with her (her giggle, especially the supressed one is infectious), as she would be to tell you off for pomposity or whatever. Once, a Very Important Person came to stay overnight. It was Hamatan in Ibadan, the chilly, bone dry wind that blows for a few weeks around January and February from the Sahara bringing with it layers and layers of dust on everything, polished furniture included. You can't dust it every day, for each time you do, you risk scratching the polish, as if you'd lightly run a gentle sandpaper over it. The Important Visitor idly wiped his finger over a coffee-table top and looked at it disapprovingly. It wasn't aggressive, just an idle gesture during conversation; but it was rude. My mother pursed her lips in a way that portended a storm, clenched her jaw which portended that the storm was not to be violent, got up, left the room, returned moments later with a duster which she handed without comment to the instantly chastened Important Person.

Life was much harder back at home in England after we left Liberia. It is an old pattern. It wasn't, really, until they managed to buy an old house, Cae Du, literally just off the beaten track in Snowdonia and ran there for a few years, a guest house, that such happiness possessed during the West African years returned. They were very good at that, too, mostly for a reason I am aiming at and will mention last, but also because they could talk to anyone at any level, because my mother was an excellent cook, and my father, more limited as a cook, was nevertheless an excellent roast chef: turkey, potatoes, Sunday roast, and bread as it happens. And my mother kept and keeps a clean, orderly, warm and lived-in home, which in this case, she simply shared with her guests.

My father grew ill, and for the last few years of his life required constant attendance and care. My mother bore the brunt of this of course, but Adrian and his wife Sue lived not far off and took a large share of the burden. In his last months Keith was bedridden and towards the end, barely conscious, an almost invisible twitch at one comer of his mouth, a tiny pressure from an unmoving thumb was all the communication there was, though it was clear that he heard and understood. So that when he died in the smallest hours of the morning, in the arms of his wife and sons, for my mother grief was mixed with utter exhaustion.

Those are the main points of Liz's biography the reader might find useful in reading what follows. There is one characteristic of my mother's, however, that I do not want to leave out, even while it will be obvious to anyone reading these letters. And that is her wisdom, in particular her deep, intuitive, and pretty much infallible understanding of people. Coupled with her very wide experience, this means that she is an excellent counsellor and advisor, and has been to young and old for decades. She has no education to speak of, but was taught to love books and poetry by a teacher (may God rest his soul) who gave up his lunch hours to read poetry with interested pupils, a legacy she passed on to we boys in long evenings reading to us: Tennyson, Matthew Arnold, some speeches or sonnets from Shakespeare, Browning, the Bible, a bit of Milton or Wordsworth, Keats, Kipling, occasionally a novel spread over many weeks, some bits of some Churchill speeches.

My father's greatest worry was what would happen to my mother when once he was gone, how she would manage without him. When he mentioned it to me, which he often did, I consoled him as best I could; but what I really wanted to do was to laugh. I don't know where he had been all these years, but it would be far more appropriate to wonder what would have happened to him, how he would have managed without her if she had gone first. We children all thought so. These letters tell the story differently. But the support, the care was always mutual; my parents, for all the ups and downs of their marriage, the tempests and the calms in the dog days, my parents loved each other in the old-fashioned sense; they were united as one. Take half of one away and only half remains whatever the 'one' might be.

My father was much less obvious than my mother: where she was outspoken, he was reserved. But he had charisma and strength: however quietly he would enter a crowded room heads would turn to see what had just happened. When he died, there was a pause, and then we instinctively opened a window wide, and you felt the personality leave the house; you could see and feel the light go out of the rooms; it doesn't come back on. Speaking for myself, I waited for it for years before I realised that that was just how the world was now, it changes, you find a different balance and adjust to the new world. My mother's finding or making a new balance and a new, at least partial wholeness is what is recorded in these letters.

My mother asked me to take charge of editing this manuscript because she knew that as an academic I had edited things before. But it is really a team effort of my brothers (Gordon and Adrian) and our sister Elizabeth Goyder, who appears often in the letters, usually as 'Dr Liz', and me. Mostly the editing involved assigning a few fugitive dates and places, the usual corrections of spelling and punctuation, the occasional grammar tweak, adding a word or two to make clear to readers not

Editor's Preface

family one or two things we take for granted. But everything after this preface is my mother's words, virtually untouched, except for a poem of Keith's printed at the back. There are some rearrangements of parts I have made which I'll explain in a moment, and all names not immediate family have been changed and one or two place-names ditto. My mother preferred not to have any part in it after she had finished the writing, and, rather later the Preface: too close to emotions still raw, and this explains a few places where I have inserted a comment like 'Liz appears to mean ...', rather than asking her outright: 'Mummy, what do you mean here?' I have left Liz's dates just the way she wrote them, only correcting the odd slip, because the variations are sometimes significant and because as they are they, too, reflect something of her state of mind and personality.

I have brought some passages to the front to give the reader an indication of the sort of thing which awaits them. I have done this because there are at the opening of the manuscript some pages of mere jottings as my mother struggles to find an outlet, and to find her feet and mental stability after the main prop of her life was removed. I have left these in because this book is, without my mother having realised it until much later, not only about my father, Keith, but an unconscious odyssey of my mother's from almost complete prostration to the relative stability of her own two feet. In the end she bids my father farewell, realising and at last able to do so, that she must, that she may, now make her own life, to look forward and not backwards.

Editor's Preface

This was not originally intended to be published, or even read by anyone. As the reader will see, my mother began to think the family might want to read it after she had gone, but eventually she came to realise that perhaps her own journey might help others to make theirs, just as her reading of the similar journeys of others before her, helped her. And so it is that I find myself writing a preface to, a sort of forwarding address on, an intimate, private manuscript first addressed to my father, and now forwarded to those who might find some light for their own feet trudging as it may be a strait and dusty road of their own. But as A.E. Housman said, that road will eventually guide you back, even if it takes you round the whole world to do so. ('White in the Moon …' from *A Shropshire Lad*.)

Tübingen 21st January, 2022   Julian Lethbridge

Author's Preface

We enter into the world of death – whether we want to or not. At some time in our own life we are touched by death – a friend or a relative – it is always there. This is not a story of death but of the dying and of picking up life again. "Till death us do part" – and it did. At 76 and after a long illness it is a natural happening and I thought 'Yes I can cope', until I realised that death had taken away half of me at the same time as it took Keith. It is not just one of us who dies.

The words – death, dead, widow, bereft, relict – are horrible, horrible words, and their meanings make you want to weep. I know because I looked them up, because this situation was not real for me. The meanings of the words were very real.

A story of a relationship from 17-76 and of my husband's death and my journey into a life as a relict.

After a long life together we thought as many do that retirement would be our time.

When does one of the brain illnesses start? Does one know or sense? Like a lot of people, I think we can only see in retrospect, and it is in retrospect that I see our troubles started a long time before we had a 'real' diagnosis. Here I am talking about at least 5 years before we had a name for it.

We had a business, having bought an old Welsh farmhouse croft up a mountain in Snowdonia [in

North Wales] which we lovingly and with great pleasure restored, and it became a very real home in the hills – to which visitors came. For 12 years we worked here and had lots of fun.

But we were getting older and physically tired. So we sold. At least we thought we had – packed, with Pickfords coming on Monday – contracts to be signed on Friday – and they withdrew.

Looking back, I believe that was the catalyst for Keith's problem. An easy-going man who really liked people – suddenly our world had collapsed, and we didn't actually let the anger out – we should have ranted and raved – all of which wouldn't have changed things, but maybe we internalised too much. We unpacked, but had either given away or sold so much, no way could we still trade – so 2 years of stress and strain, and we both changed.

Keith became bad-tempered, not at all part of his nature – we quarrelled – life became less of a blessing.

And his health started to break down. Just his eyesight was affected but surgery made that better. He'd been a diabetic for years, though under control, but now that altered.

One of our three sons said to me 'Mum, have you noticed that Dad's hands shake?' I said I had and thought it was Parkinson's but I didn't want him to know at this time. Later, when he had a diagnosis he was very angry that I hadn't told him – which only goes to show that in life we make many mistakes, not always are they reversible. After seeing three consultants it was diagnosed and along with it cancer of the prostate and a heart valve deficiency.

So what follows are the letters I wrote to him after death. I nursed him at home for many years and at his death we were all with him, just holding him but letting him go.

After 60 years of being together I was lost and one day I wanted so much to tell him I loved him and missed him that I started writing – as if he would answer.

Now, two years later, I know that for me that was absolutely the right thing to do. Although these letters will go to my sons and their families – I do hope they also help you if you should come to read them.

Looking back, I can see that at first, I had no coherent thought, no grammar, no sentences. I leave these almost incoherent scratchings in the beginning of this little book, because they are my first weak efforts to talk to this 'nothing', to get to him, to grab him back – perhaps to grab myself back, I don't really know.

The sick are not romantic, not really... It's a different sort of love that puts up with illness. Old love.

(*The Right Attitude to Rain*, Alexander McCall Smith, p 85.)

Our commitment was for better or worse and I'm fulfilling the promise that both of us made. When I sit and look back and think what fun we've had – but now I'm a nurse, a mother, not a wife or lover anymore; these roles have changed, it's very sad that you can't continue until your dying day being in love in the same way. But we are still together and there's enough of both of us left to enjoy what we can.

(Liz Lethbridge, BBC, Silverville, Episode 2, broadcast 5th August, 2009.)

Letters to Keith

Friday 11th September

I had a dream – 3 weeks after Keith died. Keith was in trouble – what trouble I don't know – sinking or something like that – and I was fighting to get to him. Fighting obstacles and people to get to them out of the way. And I did get to him and held him and wouldn't let anything hurt him again – and for some reason I remember him wearing a yellow shirt as I grabbed him back from danger.

My worry since he died has been did I do enough? Should I have spent more time with him – offered him more help – massaged him more.

Do I still feel numb or am I just generally an unfeeling person?

If asked did I love him, I would say yes – vehemently – but what is love? When he was dying I kept saying, I love you so much, and I do and did. But now? How can you love 'nothing' no person, no body, no speech, no reciprocation. Is love just this awful dull ache?

* * *

13.7.09

Read love story

Lovely lady

? their wedding vows – Better – worse

Nurses – improvised and caring

Commitment

The influence you have had darling – goes beyond the grave.

My brain is soft and floppy, doesn't hold anything – dates, times, events

They are always floating around but I can't anchor them.

The sea of emptiness is just flowing around with little buoys cluttering around and no ability to link them together to make a complete whole.

RSW called, she needs encouragement, the world is full of so many people who are not whole – or even halfway whole.

Pin drop in hall.

Showing True Love

Hugs, Extra Care, lifted it up to show what compassion is.

You would have been so pleased that you'd helped so many people.

20 + people, how it helped them – respect and admire – through us to God

15.7.09

Today, choked.

Letter from Hilary, full of love and care, makes me want to howl but of course I can't.

God is good and is leading me somewhere but I don't know where

July 2009

Catia said, many young people will be jealous of that relationship (Keith's and mine), Lord has this been used by you for many.

12.8.09

Starting to make notes and memories. It was tough watching the film of Keith. [BBC Silverville, Episode 2 (broadcast 5th August, 2009)]

To continue coping one couldn't let oneself see things as they really are. My poor dear man. Inner pain that he rarely showed – pain in his heart and head – the pain of the body was nothing to the inner pain.

15th Upton House – Art

Miss having bottom patted.

Saturday 15th, August 2009

It amazed me that a young person – 20+ said that a lot of young people would be jealous of our relationship (Re: the film)

Are we so different from what we had thought?

Monday, 17th August, 2009

Went to grave.

Much tidier now, primroses hanging on. I did cry but it's as if my tears are rationed – but I need to howl from my toe upwards – will I ever be able to let this lot go? It's a big, big weight.

I'm sure people think that 'Liz is laughing etc. – must be OK.' But this weight I can't move – is always there.

Colour coding ideas

Love Life death etc.

Village diary???

August 2009

Sat 22nd August 2009
Prayed for guidance
All the boys pushing and pushing me to write.
Julian giving me framework
Spent time with Alex and Michael.

Sunday 23rd August
I miss Keith. Doing some reading about Africa and it started me remembering our life there, feel body mind and spirit. Now Keith is dead – so am I in a different way.

It was so good to have our African friends to sing to Keith when he was alive and then at his grave and this for me.

Today I am nearer crying than before – partly I think because my sleeping is so bad. I'm so tired. Body mind and spirit. I miss you darling.

(Notes to self)

Africa. Zimbabwe (SA.)

Widows welcomed into circle

Fathers – sons – Widows understand.

'Can You Drink the Cup'?? Henri Nouwen

Keep wanting to turn and talk to Keith! "Look darling".

24th August 09
This has been an awful day. I feel as though I'm halfway dead. Even thinking is difficult – my head is full of tears.

But I got through it. 10:30. I'm going to bed. I hope to sleep. Adrian and Sue took me shopping to spend money I haven't got. Shall I write 'Letters to my Lover?'

28th August

Today I do not feel so dragged down – a little more life.

Arranged for change of telephone.

Adrian's b'day

29th August

Very tired – heavy

Got up early – watered garden

Went back to bed and slept could do with more.

Bill is inviting me to attend talk Christopher Martin Jenkins [Much loved BBC Test Match Special commentator]; said I would tell 'Keith'.

Death – dead is becoming more real.

30th August

Today. My first trip on my own by taxi. Managed everything. All I bought has to go back – I am fat.

Shall I write about "The Adventure of Death".

I always wanted another "adventure".

This would for all of us be the 'last' one.

Confucius he say: one day at a time.

So what it my coping today?

September 2009

1st September
London. with silver cup. Interesting – my thoughts etc.

Also, was Cae Du a training ground for later, e.g. Keith's illness?

2nd September
Drawing class a PLUS. Interest in history of art, brilliant. My brain will be used!

3rd September
War declared 70 years ago

Went to antique place [Brackley] with Carrie and I brought lovely chair for desk. Lovely to see so much of one's past.

4th September
Went to Alex – glad she's taking time out for herself. Michael was OK. when she got back.

5th September
A very busy day.

Coffee at Alex's

Lunch at Alex's and Michael and Gavin.

Alex rang could she come down. She needs to have time out – but to accept that Michael needs her love – willingly given.

Helene and Eileen came. Nice to see them.

Sunday 6th September
Thank the Lord that my life (this week anyway) is getting bigger – but …

Bookcases moved etc.
Why am I so busy?
Putting things off?

Monday 7th

What shall I write? What am I here for? What shall I do?

Then God says "The Past, The Future". Write.

Fine, but still how do I start?

Must make more of a picture – ambience – description, etc.

So me, the person I still am – am going on a journey – backwards – and then hopefully forward – to who knows what.

Just now my brain is soft and flabby. Needs exercise tonight.

Childhood – work / love / children / Africa / illness / caring

Keith died

After years. 4-5 things wrong.

Describe the place and coping mechanism.

Sept 9

Had a good evening – discussion on Spirituality in Psyche

Having few published – ? Julian

Sept 10

Lee and I had coffee together here. A lovely lady, wise and kind. Touched on many subjects.

Out to shop with Alex. Lunch and then shopping – back to clearing up and then off to "bar" and ladies. Good evening and group of ladies at coffee bar.

Sept 11

Read my worship book in bed this am. Very painful so didn't want to get out of bed.

I read about one's sense of identity – this rings true for me because of Keith's death. Also listened to programme – 6 widows various ages and how they coped, all said that when the pain had gone – they realised for the first time they were "ME".

Interesting thought as to where "ME" was.

Friday 11th September

Almost entirely different reactions to film – TV (Silverville) – to what we expected. It seems to have helped people who are not sick but those who need role models for living our relationship. Keith would be so happy that even now his life would still be of use. If we had been film stars, I think the response would please us – "an overnight hit" after years of working. I'm so pleased and again very humbled.

Friday 11th September

I had a dream – 3 weeks after Keith died. He was in trouble – what trouble I don't know – sinking or something like that – and I was fighting to get to him. Fighting obstacles and people to get to them out of the way and I did get to him and held him and wouldn't let anything hurt him again – and for some reason I remember him wearing a yellow shirt as I cuddled him and as I grabbed him back from danger.

My worry since he died has been, did I do enough? Should I have spent more time with him – offered him more help – massaged him more.

Today I felt much more at peace – calmer – and I believe this dream helped me.

I did do all I could. I fought for him – and protected him so his passing was easier. He did die, but at peace – not frightened and alone.

I thank God for this dream – I had a replay of what I actually did for Keith but really was too close to see what level I was working at. Somehow the dream helped me see what I have done – I have fought for him, I have protected him.

Saturday 12th September

Not a good night, tired and on edge. Miserable day, and Keith is not here.

Do I still feel numb or am I just generally an unfeeling person?

I am glad Keith is not here, because why should he continue to be in pain – unnecessarily – what good was it doing anyone – especially him. But I don't really remember the man. It has been years that I have been his nurse, his carer, do I really remember him as a person? I look at his photo and his laughing. Did I see him laughing, or was it my own fatigue that wore him down. Oh dear, so many questions now to be answered, perhaps not, even from the other side of the grave.

If asked did I love him, I would say yes – vehemently – but what is love? When he was dying I kept saying, I love you so much, and I do and did.

But now? How can you love 'nothing' no person, no body, no speech, no reciprocation. Is love just this awful dull ache?

How do we love God, or our understanding of God. To love is to think and interact with the person, but if they are not there … .

This is probably going into philosophy and that doesn't help with coping – missing, wondering about this person whom you loved as a tangible being.

Today I'm sad, because I looked at a photo of this person – my personal friend, lover, protector – and he is not here and my feelings are sad, lonely Should I really be enjoying having more space, less medical equipment around, or do I only want that pain-filled body in the next room, to whom I could speak, and touch, even if he couldn't respond? For him, of course not, but what about me? He is at peace at last, and I am in pain. 57 years, what can erase that knowledge, laughter? Time, no I don't think so. Maybe the ache gets less, I hope so. But what if one has no hope of a life after death, where we should know each other again.

What a great big hole that must leave.

How does one cope with that?

Thank God Keith and I do believe and we do have hope – but the emptiness of now is still here to cope with. A stunned feeling – an emptiness – a constant – oh Keith, look at this – or we must do or see or go to such and such.

'Quoth the raven "nevermore" ' [Edgar Allan Poe, 'The Raven']

Sept 12

Gordon took me to the grave and we have agreed, as with Adrian that the edging etc. would be best for Keith's grave.

I'm so impressed – and helped – reading Henri Nouwen that he can't remember his past childhood and youth.

It isn't just me!

Do I write back from here – now – Dart around or have a framework?

Maybe the beginning of writing?

Sept 13

Quote from Freya Starke, at 90 years.

"What's beyond?" 'No, life is a series of new horizons – you reach out and find there's another – just beyond.'

Death will be like that – an horizon that you can actually step off and there you are."

(Death) Peaceful quiet restful

My thoughts?

What do I think?

How do you feel?

Could write to Keith

Life will be fine in 2009. Well its three quarters gone and I do not find it fine

Sept 13

Very tired after yesterday waking but went to boot sale – good antique reference books. Must remember to keep book of quotes re: Freya Starke at 90 (?)

15th Sept

Spoke to BBC today, let them know the positives from the film. Marjory and Liam said I should write. I want to but I just can't get started.

Lots of pain today.

Rosemary told me to read 2 Corinthians 4 tell (show) others how to cope (with God).

Marjory said to let her have anything I write! I do so need guidance – and I am aware that I'm frightened of being rejected. Before I die I would like to do something. What I don't know. I need to be shown – I can't see – sic Catherine Marshall. Everyone thinks I'm the same me – only less tired! I'm not. I'm a changed woman – behaving like a child – "don't know what to do" etc.

Sept 16

I think I may be guilty of displacement – because I deep down, don't want to get started. Not something I want to do – and me getting rejected. Went to art class – gossip – not something I want to do. Need teaching – not talking.

Sept 17

Went back to bed. Keith woke me up! "Oh there you are". It was the voice of Keith – a long time ago. I knew it was my imagination, but it was good to hear him.

Still no internet.

Went to Thursday group – do enjoy just chatting. Ruby is obviously better, she takes care of me! Meeting others is nice as well

September 2009

Sept 18

Bad night – bad dreams.

Everyone angry and shouting, no one looking after me and caring about me. (Should analyse?).

Meeting with John, Graham and others.

I really must try not to talk too much. I say things that make me look a fool, at least that's what I think – after I've said them.

Pain so bad today I had to go and have a massage, feels much better. Alex still having trouble with Michael's leg bag.

Sept 19

Alex is in a bad way today – she really does need outside help.

Sept 20

Six months ago Keith died – and I still don't have a purpose – I read a lot and keep busy, but in a drifty sort of way. Am I just lonely?

Whatever my future will be – it really can't be too physical – my hips and knees hurt badly.

So it will have to be – of the mind. Writing – that's what I'd like to do.

Songs of Praise singing from Wales, made me cry. I miss Keith more now than at the beginning – does it really take time to sink in?

Have watched a lot of TV this weekend. Mostly because of Agatha Christie. Must not become an addict!

September 2009

Sept 21

Don't know why, but yesterday and today I am just – very tired and in pain – but also very tearful, feel absolutely full. I miss Keith a lot – but why tears now??

Anything – not even related to Keith makes me want to blub.

Did first singing lesson today and going to chat tonight. I'm afraid I'll sound like a frog – an old frog.

The women are very caring of me. It's as though I've been taken into a circle, it's nice.

September 20th, Sunday

I'm adrift. I'm perched here in bed, with a really bad head, but no plans for the day. Adrift really, no aim, no purpose, no reason to move and do anything, yet I am a doer.

What does God want from me. I can't even rest physically, nothing to aim at. Just holding my head and wondering which painkiller to take next. Can't even find cause and effect to alleviate the pain.

Maybe I'll just get up and go for a walk.

Good morning darling.

I've just been thinking over our life together all 59 of them.

6 months ago, in our apartment at Lovat Fields you said your final goodbye to me and the family – peaceful and calm and the family.

People have said often to me in our life what a close family we are, but what does close mean? In and out of each other's pocket. No. If we really think about it, I think it's respect. The boys for us and us for them.

September 2009

Let's go back a bit and see what we think about life – and in your case now Death – but that comes to us all eventually. I have obviously to write from my point of view, but do but in if you want. (I wish).

We've always enjoyed talking haven't we? Me after getting wound up, and you calming me down. (Very irritating calm people can be!)

Sept 22
Can't get a digital hearing aid, my ear canal is too small. Wish the rest of me was small!

Did John Lewis shopping today. Was good to go with a mind of what I want.

Alex had her tests today – results on Friday.

Dr Liz rang tonight. My feelings and weepiness are quite normal. The subconscious adjusting to a great loss of part of my life. I have worried, dropping things, etc. Adrian the same – relief for both of us. Easier for me than him.

Sept 23
Again – slept badly then woke up late. 1st singing lesson proper! Janet, I really will try – prayers, drawing, singing, writing – I must make some sort of order out of all this, as well as exercise for my hip/leg whatever, pain very bad today.

Much better if I rest then do something, but walking is very painful. It helped talking to Liz last night. This is all part of natural grieving – as she said 'a very large part of you has been taken away from you'. The subconscious is working hard to get you in balance again.

Today I am internetted and broadbanded. Hope I can work it.

Sept 24

Dr this morning – he thinks I will need a hip replacement. Hearing aid, new hip. Thank goodness I still have my teeth.

Well at least I can now work on what to do about the pain.

Firstly, I must lose some weight, that always helps.

Alex is absolutely shattered again. Once she's got the results of her test maybe they'll be able to do something to help both of them.

Sept 26 Saturday

Alex's results show her Thyroxine is low. Cholesterol high. Heart okay.

No pills or potions, first walk more.

Sara's birthday today, haven't seen her because she's off doing something.

I must do something about writing. I'll try to do the three pages a day and see what comes to light.

Yes, I'd like something published, but it is more a definition of me. I have done something, I have some standing, all nebulous, but real to me.

It's been a nice quiet restful day, I have enjoyed today, not just got through it. The reason, I think partly that I have been on my own most of the day, giving me time to admire the changing colours of autumn. Beautiful this year.

This year with you not here – (I'm not busy now) I begin to realise that I'm also in the autumn of my years. Where did they come from?

Be nice to leave something beautiful behind when I fall off my twig! [Keith's Poem printed at the back of this book.]

Sept 27

Woke up with quite a lot of pain in my hip. Today is absolutely beautiful, and I would like to go for a walk, but I can't, must go and sit in the garden which is a pleasure, everything looks so good.

The peace and quiet here is amazing considering we are at a crossing of a major road. Just the hum of traffic which I don't mind, at least it says there is a life out there, beyond the closeness of our quite small apartment, which I have to say is ample and I couldn't wish for anything better. It's just having been used to big houses that makes it appear small. Certainly, having the garden makes it feel much bigger.

Julian rang. Good chat about Plato, thinking, etc. The way forward for me, don't know. But I find good conversation is so important.

Sept 28

I've got shingles, which partly explains why I feel so down. Just hope it doesn't go onto my face. So the next few days (? weeks) must try to build myself up a little. But as always, good to know what you're working with. Adrian and Sue have moved stuff in the study and now I have the computer up and running.

Did lots of reading on shingles – after the years of looking after you, which I have no regrets about. My own body is saying, Right, now can I have a rest?

Sept 29

Keith's birthday.

I can't remember last year but I am alone on this the first birthday after his death. Adrian and Sue are taking me to the grave. Why? I don't know except I just can't let him be on his own today. I have to tell him I love him.

Being maudlin is not my style but there are some things other people won't or can't understand and these are private thoughts and feelings special to each of us. So today – it is also a beautiful day and I shall just be near the last place I left Keith.

As I walked toward the grave I was so pleased. The primroses I planted for Keith – there was one solitary flower – just for him on his birthday. Lovely.

Sept 30

It is cooler today, I'm glad about that because my shingle blisters itch – much worse if it's warm.

Sitting in the study writing this is really nice. The room looks good, it's light and bright and our "Low" [David Low] cartoons make me smile. I do wish you could see the house now darling, you'd like it and I think would approve of the changes I've made.

You might not like the look of me though, I look as though I've got scurvy and it's beginning to be really painful on the nerve pathway.

Eileen sent me down a meal, but is worried about offending me. I told her to offend me as much as she likes!

I have, and it's hard to admit, enjoyed my day in bed. Certainly I have no desire to 'do' anything, so that helps.

That little primrose from yesterday makes me smile. I think it bloomed for Keith. Gwyn says it's Keith telling me everything is okay. Whatever – it was a lovely blessing.

Eileen and Alex have visited to make sure I'm okay, and loaning me books. Can't find my glasses though. My head feels swollen and is continually sore.

Tomorrow I will rest again, on the Friday Gordon is coming, that will be good. He reminds me so much of you darling – "cuddly teddy bear".

October 2009

Oct 1

It's a lovely day. The autumn freshness but still lots of warm sun.

Fortunately, the wind has dropped which means the plants will last another day without water. I really don't have any strength for carrying heavy watering cans.

Next year I will get rid of the hostas and just have trees and shrubs.

Although Keith and I have always loved hostas I can't keep up with watering all the time. Our age changes, our bodies change, so I think for me now, the garden has to change.

Must buy the biggest pots I can and then I don't need to worry so much about watering.

Sometimes I feel like Quasimodo [Victor Hugo, Hunchback of Notre-Dame, 1831] I'm lop-sided from carrying cans of water.

Oct 3

Yesterday, Gordon came, only for a few hours, but it was good to see him. He finished the work on the computer so now it's up and running.

The hostas have all gone, that's sad but I have to reorganise the garden otherwise it's too much work.

Thought I felt better for a couple of hours but, oh boy I didn't, and today I certainly don't. I'm frightened it's going to affect my eye/brain, and of course we have no surgery today.

Today is the first really cold day we've had and I've put the heating on, lots of leaves everywhere. Reminds me of Keith's poem. I miss him. Even if he was ill he was the other part of my life, no, it really doesn't seem as though I have a life, just living.

Oct 4

In pain, don't feel well and blisters everywhere

Oct 5

Sitting here waiting to be connected to the Dr. Feel awful, arm losing its use and skill, as if it's been smashed.

Oct 8

Not writing because I feel rotten. Shingles pain and tanked to eyeballs on tablets, lovely day though, sunshine and water butt full.

Can't sleep! And it's midnight.

Just watched a programme about T.S. Eliot. "In my end is my beginning."

(Can this be a metaphor for me? My life now without Keith?) As "My life began with Keith." Maybe a new life now? A beginning is the end. Who knows.

Oct 9

Went shopping today with Alex. She is tired and very weary. It's like looking at myself when Keith was alive, but I did seem to have more support than she does.

Lovely story of Michael kissing her arm at night. Thank God for love, one and the love of God for us and to us.

Reading Henri Nouwen. "Oughts and Shoulds." Keep thinking of human life and all the things I 'ought' to do, go, visit etc. Then if we don't do these things then we repine. I should have etc. No peace either way.

Thoughts are begging to come, I do want to write.

Oct 10 Saturday

Stayed in bed for quite a while today as I don't feel that well.

Head bones ache as if bruised, glands up and everything hurts.

Still reading Rosie Swale, I think I have the stirrings of wanting to write.

"Till death do us part" and it did.

After 59 years of knowing and loving each other, we were parted.

You were tired and had suffered enough you wanted to go.

We didn't want to lose you but we let you go, because you would be free of pain and at peace.

Our blessing was, and I like to think it was for you too, that we the boys, and I were there with you and each touching you and telling you that we loved you, and you went and we said goodbye.

I think our grief at that part was eased because, you 'The Essence' of my man and the boys' father had been going over the past 4-5 years.

This and our belief in a life after death has carried us through.

Its now 7 months since you died, it's a Saturday night. I'm just getting over shingles.

I have a blinding headache and in spite of a sleeping tablet, I can't sleep, and my mind and body miss you.

Little memories of our life together keep popping up and I am sad and tired and I want you, you who would always say to me "don't worry, it will be alright."

The thing is I understand who and what you were more now you're dead. I think I begin to see you as a person, as people outside us saw you, people often say to me how they miss your sense of humour and lovely smile.

How or what do they think I miss and feel?

C.S. Lewis LOVE!

17-77 is a long time, more than some people's lifetime, and that is what we had. It just doesn't seem possible that all that life could have been ours together and yet it seems so short.

You saw me at 17 remember, and wanted me, but we didn't meet until a year or so later, and you still wanted me, but I couldn't stand you!

What's that saying about hate being akin to love? (photo, us = the boys). I do love you darling.

I'm going back to bed again to try to get some sleep, my heart and my head ache, I need sleep.

Oct 11 Sunday

A day I would like to hurry up and go. I'm in so much pain today with this shingles and no pain killers seem to touch it.

When you were in pain I do hope you got some relief. I hate the thought of your suffering, but I did all I could to alleviate it. Dr's, nurses, all of them were there for you.

However, this pain will pass and I shall still be here, and missing you like mad.

Oct 12 Monday

Do you remember in Africa, when you had typhoid and I had malaria, your temperature was 105 and I couldn't stop shaking with malaria and I cold sponged you, to get your temperature down? We both thought you were going to die – the only difference was, you didn't care and I did. So many things have happened to us haven't they, we've laughed and cried about together. Remember waking up from that, both of us in bed, to find half the church members by our bed? Praying for us. We thought we'd died and gone to heaven! But we both got better, it took you longer though.

Remember in Nigeria we drove north up to Jos on the plateau for you to recuperate in the cool air. Much less humid up there.

It was beautiful, just so different and the Hausa people were so good to us.

My abiding memory of Jos is on the way North, stopping at the government rest house (mud hut) overnight and seeing the Milky Way and hearing donkeys bray all night. That really was magical.

The boys' best memory and ours really was swimming in a warm river. We swimming on one bank and the baboons having their morning drink and wash on the other.

Oct 12

Shall I continue writing to you darling? Do you want to go down memory lane?

Our boys think I should, they want to read it too. Their life and ours.

But where do I start? When we first met? You always remembered that occasion better than me.

You even remembered what I wore, mind you so did I, but I didn't know you were looking then. The hat comes particularly to mind. A Robin Hood type of hat with a long feather. I think it was beige, how peculiar. I never asked you what colour it was. Fortunately, I've always liked hats and you've always liked me wearing them, even from 17 years old.

When was that, probably – 50-51 ish. Now 2009. No I can't believe what life we've had and now it's just me, Moi.

How could we describe our love?

There was passion, there was sexy love passion, but overall a love that was like rolling up in a duvet and going to sleep, a warm comforting love. That was always there, always just next to either of us. How do you describe love anyway? Think it was [William] Blake who said 'seek not to tell thy love, love that never told can be.'

And yet that is what I am trying to do. I just love you and I know I was deeply loved by you.

When at the end you couldn't even speak we were blessed with that few minutes when your voice came back and we had just a few minutes' conversation and we could tell each other 'I love you very much.' That was such a blessing.

So my darling, we loved, we do love and have been loved. What more could we ask.

I'm now off to take my painkiller and hopefully sleep. At least you won't catch my shingles. I sincerely hope no one does catch it from me.

Herrick "What is love?"

'Love is a circle that doth restless move
In the sweet eternity of love'

I'm quoting poetry at you because I have always liked poetry. You didn't but I remember your Mum saying "I knew Keith was in love, he was sitting outside reading poetry."

Having said that, you did of course towards the end of your life write some good pieces. One in particular had the staff in tears, and then the one you wrote for me, when you were first diagnosed, "You are the wind under my wings." [Printed at the back of the book.]

This morning Adrian took me to the Dr's, I'm to double my dose of painkillers. Probably no sense out of me for the next few days, but maybe I'll sleep.

Next day:

Yes I did, sleep that is, and woke feeling much more human but decided that my life now doesn't necessitate getting up at the crack of dawn, so I sank back onto my pillows and read, R.S. Thomas, and in there it tells of his marriage to Elsi and their reception at the Goat in Bala, and I turned to tell you! I do this quite often. We've always enjoyed telling each other 'little bits'.

Write more and in detail about memories. The going to Meredith and Cae Du – rook for the garden.

Actually, I'm going down to Wales this weekend with Carrie in her car, and going to church in Bala. 4 years ago since we left there, but it was the right move, you were looked after better here. I couldn't have nursed you all that time on my own. Doors open, doors close.

October 2009

Thursday Oct 15. Wales.

Tonight darling I am in a big double bed that almost needs a stool to stand on to leap onto the mattress. The house is large and we've been here often, but never to sleep. I'm at Gwyn's, she picked me up from Betws-y-Coed and Carrie carried on to Anglesey. It was a good journey, and remembering that for quite a few years this area was our home. Coming down some of these little lanes and seeing the gorgeous autumn colours, you would have loved it. I haven't seen 'Cae Du' yet, our home in the mountains, we got here in the dark. It feels like coming home.

And now I'm in the lovely old bed. I feel like the pictures of the princess and the pea, it was Dafydd's aunt's bed so probably I would think, judging by the style, Edwardian with wardrobe to match. When I arrived I saw a photo of Dafydd at a wedding. The world has been cruel to you both. Good, intelligent men and for you to have it taken away from you and for Gwyn and I to watch our men disappear. Two widows with the same memories.

That of course is why Gwyn and I can and have built on our friendship. We both wish our two men were here with us, but you had our hearts and we had yours. You would love this bed, we could cuddle and love and not fall out. I shall go to sleep now, and tomorrow see some of our past again.

(Notes to self)
Wales – first time, boys at camp, grass snake

Love, Remembrance, Cae Du (new owners), Meredith X 2

Pride, Humility, Tears, (?)

Books, Christchurch, Memories

Weekend laughing and crying, Gwyn and I 'ghost' on stairs

Maes y Neuadd, (?) Remember our [?]loft

Opera, crying, weekend of tears

Widows, circle, another club

Trees, Offertory

Monday 19th Oct

Oh darling,

I've had such a good break, staying with Gwyn, and love has been shown to me and people's comments about you and what you've done for others, my heart soul, mind – whatever – has been lifted, and I've felt so close to you in Wales looking at 'our' mountains that surrounded us and, oh, the fresh air.

There's so much I want to tell you, that if you could you would have a good laugh.

Carrie took me down on her way to Anglesey. I got picked up in Betws-y-Coed and the fun started. Gwyn and I just get on so well together, actually the weekend passed in and laughs for both of us.

It's about 5 years since Dafydd died, but the heart still aches. I'm sure we don't ever feel whole again, maybe just a little healed as time goes on.

The mountains of Wales have, in a way, with their height and strength, lifted me, and the wonderful warm welcome, quite took my breath away. To see the same houses, streets, people, was so good, and they were delighted in seeing me and remembering you.

On Sunday morning we drove from Llan to Bala, Gwyn and I, through all the ways we knew so well, mountains, lakes, dropping down the hill and climbing again, past our old house and parked the car in the school park Ysgol Berwyn and then into the church.

The re-ordering has been beautifully done, everywhere is so light and inviting. I wish you could have seen it, I know you would have just loved it.

You got a special prayer said for you and I had the most warm and cuddly welcome.

Oct 24

It's a week ago since I saw the mountains of Wales and inhaled the clear, clean air, but just some things I want to tell you.

Before I do though, a lovely thought I came across when reading this week. A woman losing a loved friend, 'He was dead – I accepted that. Now suddenly I realized he was no longer alive, and somehow that's not quite the same thing.' And she cried. [*Pig in a Passage*, Anne Drysdale, 1997]

That is just how I felt. I was there when you died, I saw it happen, I can't gainsay that. But for you no longer to be around and near me, that is pain, heartache, loneliness, and all I can say is 'I love you darling' not, I still love you, but I do love you, that doesn't leave when you do.

In fact, I have more time to love you now you're gone.

Those last years, when all my energies were used in keeping you comfortable, your spirits up and as pain-free as possible, didn't leave much energy for loving, only as I cared for you, that was showing my love.

But now, as everyone does, if only ..., maybe ..., I should have done this/that.

There didn't seem to be time to just hold your hand and 'love you', this I regret not seeing before, I'm sorry.

To go back to my break. Gwyn took me to the WNO (Welsh National Opera) singing La Traviata. I don't know why I hadn't realized this was the story of someone dying of TB! Probably I should have chosen the alternative which was Butterfly, but it's the one opera I can't stand.

Still, I think the quiet controlled sniffing did me good, unleashed some of the stiff British upper lip-coping mechanism.

We laughed together though, Gwyn hadn't got a tissue so used the end of her scarf! She told me she noted a few red eyes as we left. It was beautifully acted and sung. It did my soul good.

Then the next day we went to Maes y Neudd (remember we went there for afternoon tea on our wedding anniversary once).

Something I learnt this time, was that Cromwell had actually spent 2 nights there, whether on his way to Ireland or not, no one is sure. (The restaurant is now called after him).

After this trip, I have (apart from my shingles), felt mentally better.

Nothing will ever make life right again without you, but maybe delving into our past – for me anyway – is the answer to managing my life from here on.

What I want to do, if it doesn't bore you? is to remember our life, beginning, middle, and sadly, the end, as always darling I love you.

As I have always said, my life began when I met you. You formed me, strengthened me and built me up.

My childhood, you accepted I didn't want to talk about and you never ever tried to make me speak about it. That was a noble and caring part of you. You really were 'a good man'. A man of peace and integrity.

Why do we learn things when it's too late? Not that under any circumstances do I want to eulogise about you, that's not true and honest and I don't like living with falsehood.

We had some humdingers sometimes didn't we? I used to hate it when you stayed so infuriatingly calm, and then sometimes we'd forget what the argument was about and start laughing.

Today I think I understand what is meant by 'better to have loved and lost than never to have loved at all' [Tennyson, In Memorium]. We had 59 years of loving, more than some people's lifetime,

Most times its okay, but sometimes, I'm not big and strong and then the 'missing' becomes almost unbearable, but you know how I 'cope,' do something! Scrub a floor, garden, something physical, get the blood flowing, look at something beautiful and marvel.

I've just finished reading a book on R.S. Thomas, the Welsh poet. I wish you were here and we could discuss it together. Some of his poetry at the end was much softer than his early ones.

There's one there which really is the same as you've written to me. Probably why tonight I'm a bit maudlin, love you.

Good night, Nos Da ['Goodnight' in Welsh]

Going back to last night, I more and more think man's capacity for deep love is so very different to a woman's. Nothing new here. Don't remember who said – 'love to a man is a thing apart, 'tis a woman's whole existence'. Byron?

Later: Yes, Julian found it for me: Byron, *Don Juan* Canto 1, stanza CXCIV [The speaker is a woman]:

Man's love is of man's life a thing apart,
    'Tis woman's whole existence; man may range
The court, camp, church, the vessel, and the mart;
    Sword, gown, gain, glory, offer in exchange
Pride, fame, ambition, to fill up his heart,
    And few there are whom these cannot estrange;
Men have all these resources, we but one,
To love again, and be again undone.

Does that mean that because men can isolate it some way that it is deeper, whatever, in a single-minded way.

No answers, just questions.

Monday Oct 26

Last night was clock changing time and I swear every clock in the house is different. The only certainty is my watch.

Remember when we were courting and I turned up an hour early and got cross at you for being late. Me and figures/numbers again. Wonder if that teacher who rapped my knuckles at 5 'cos I couldn't do sums, knows the damage she did.

Present me with figures and I can't manage, 5-77, what do we do to each other without realising the consequences.

November 2009

Nov 1st

Had a very bad week darling. I think I hit the bottom, and, of course, when we hit the bottom we have 2 choices, lie there and whinge 'woe is me' or start climbing up. I did the latter, well I faced up to the fact that death and shingles really are not a good combination, and I did the (what I consider, the right thing) and took myself off to the Dr.

My statement that I was not depressed fell on deaf ears. He's very good, just as he was with you, and reminded me that over the last 5-6 years I'd had multiple deaths in that time!

At every stage of your destroying diseases, a part of you died, and I had to witness this and cope. You know how much I loved you and I can see his point. The man I loved died in stages, until death itself came as a release both for you and me.

Now, 7 months later, my mind and body just don't want to work, as he said, that's when shingles hit me -- no reserve. So now I'm on a course of tablets to help me sleep and relax, as the Dr said, let me help you to get well. That I found very comforting indeed.

There's also an exercise I did to help me see where I am in my life now, that I am only me. It helped me see what I can do for myself, to pick up my life again.

Nothing will ever take away the wrenching loss of you, but I have to go on. Today I did something I haven't ever done before, on my own. A walk to the restaurant and lunch, by myself. I feel incredibly brave. However, I propped a book up so that no one would sit with me! But at least I did it.

You would have been very proud of me, as you always were when I did something special.

It's time for bed now, I'm going to go and clear the kitchen then bed and a book. Good night sweetheart, love you lots.

Nov 3rd

Well, today is the start of my 'old age'! I've got a hearing aid. Everyone says it doesn't show, if only I had thicker hair.

But I have to say, I can hear, the TV is not so high. The only disturbing thing is my voice echoes back to me. But think what it must be like for those really deaf, to be able to hear again. With me it's just, as everything, age related.

Presumably it will actually be different when my brain gets the message properly.

I've been thinking about Christmas and talking with the boys, and what is going to happen (is what I myself want).

I'm having Christmas on my own. For reasons I can't properly explain I just want to have my 1st Christmas without you, just me. If I want people I've only got to go into the village, but 'I want to be alone.'

I think you would understand if the roles were reversed.

So, Christmas is going to be one you would like I think -- do what I like, eat what I like, sleep when I like, etc., etc.

So long as someone takes me to the midnight service. Remember when we went to Willen church years ago, and the Buddhist monks joined us for the Christmas service, we went back to the priory for mince pies and coffee? If only all religions and cultures mixed more – we would find much more of our human similarities rather than all our differences.

This year I will do the same as we did 25 years ago, but on my own. Without you of course I will be sad, but I think again it's another 'remembrance' to do. I believe after this and my birthday I will be able to let you go. My mind full of our life and love and fun and sorrows. But now I will be able to function as me. Do you understand that?

We've talked about dying and I know you wouldn't want me to wallow, and I am now I suppose accepting what has happened.

Adrian and Sue are taking me to the grave either Christmas Eve or Christmas Day. This is what I meant when we, you and me, talked about death. To be able to go where the last of you lies. For me that is so important. A focal point. I suppose since you've died I've been 6-7 times. Just to touch base, not every week.

When I'm writing to you like this, my love just bubbles up inside and I just wish I could say – and you hear – 'I love you so much.'

To come to a slightly less painful subject, the garden, or rather the 'terrace' no soil etc. so everything in tubs. Well I've moved the tubs containing the trees to the short piece of our L and they are, or they will be when they grow, a nice focal point as you come up to the side of the apartment.

The Choisya are the edging on the long part of the L and they are just glowing. As you and I planned the garden for next year I'm keeping to the plan as far as possible. When I sit there next summer, I will look and know you approve.

(Notes to self: Write about years of change – unrecognised illness)

Looking back though, I think the hardest part for us both on an emotional level, was when we didn't know you were ill – we thought our love had changed, we got bad tempered and snarled at each other. That put a strain on both of us and our relationship, thinking we had changed after all these years.

The strain of a changing personality was I think for me, harder than actually nursing you. For the sake of others, I hope that, soon, diagnosis can be made much earlier. Parkinson's crept up on you, then the cancer, your eyesight, everything changed you.

When you know what you're fighting it is easier. Your personality changed, and by default, so did mine. Without our past stability it would have been hard to go on.

While I am writing this I am more and more convinced that our love and our Faith is what kept us going.

I am just so sorry as are most people in a grieving state that I didn't see some more I could have done for you, like holding hands more often, couldn't cuddle because of your pain, but oh I did so love you, and still do.

I keep thinking that I might go back over our life, so many places so many people, life has been good. The only thing I wish – and we spoke about it – if only we could have gone together. But as we've always believed, happenings have a reason, its just not always easy to see at the time.

Nov 5

Had blood taken today
Then my earpiece fixed
Coffee with Alex
Wrapping presents for Santa's Grotto at the Village.

It was like being at the end of term at a girls school. Everyone talking at once, fast and loud.

Definitely must be getting old. It was nice to be part of a younger group, but I think I like seriousness rather than hilarity and mirth.

'Cantankerous old biddy.'

In their own way people do care for me and include me, that's nice.

Nov 6

Today I'm tired, dragged down, and for some reason, vaguely miserable. Maybe just not enough sleep.

Finished the evening by listening to some Gregorian Chant, so good for the soul.

Surgery rang today. Dr wants to see me. Wonder what's there. Yet another trip to the doctors, always having to get a lift.

Anyway its nearly 9and I'm off to bed.

Nov 11

Just been to hairdresser's, boy do I look better. I've been growing my hair to cover my earpiece and I looked like a scraggy old woman, now I'm still an old woman but I look more groomed.

The remembrance at the Dr's, Commemoration 11:00 am, was a very good point in the day and I'm so pleased with my blood result.

Haemoglobin fine 14

Cholesterol 4.2

Blood sugars 5

Yet I don't think this gives me licence to eat more chocolate.

Alex is very fraught today, she is near breaking point and I don't know what I can do to help.

(Notes to self): A beginning and an end.

Start of our life, episodes, travels family death and beyond for me.

A ramble thro' life, easy reading with a cuppa.

Titles.

Hello darling

From here to there and beyond.

A book of ramblings (not rambles).

Map it out!

Meeting, Keith and I.

Wales Bala, Cae Du, Abergavenny, camping Steph and Alina, Keith; Padre talk to my girls.

Lovat Fields.

Before Keith (and the beginning of life).

Or just ramble and burble, (that's more like me).

Nov 3rd

Today, first day with hearing aid. It certainly does what it says 'hearing aid' but oh it crackles and groans. However, now the TV at 9 is too loud and I sometimes had to have it at 20!

It's a beautiful autumn day, very fresh, but lovely sunshine, if winter could be like this we'd all be happy.

This is a wandering day, from one room to the next, can't settle, and I really want chocolate. Trying to diet is hard.

The boys and you would be jealous of me at the moment. I've got a ticket to go to a talk by Christopher Martin Jenkins about this year's Ashes. I know you always liked his cricket commentary. I'm going for you!

After all the years we were married I still don't understand the game, but it's full of memories – 'going to watch Daddy play.' And the cricket teas I've helped at, and remember the year I made a large cake for tea? Made it like a cricket pitch with jelly baby cricketers. I left the door of the kitchen open and Julian ate all the cricketers!

Then you had to scour Reading for more jelly babies, all we found were jelly monkeys. Our heads are full of memories but they need a kick-start. Love you. Just eaten some chocolate and lost a large filling. Oh boy, now a dentist appointment and it's such a filled tooth I suspect it will have to come out. Ah the joys of ageing, but at least we are supposed to get wiser??

Nov 5, 2009

Tonight I can't sleep. I was in bed by nine, dead tired. As soon as my head hit the pillow, ZING went my brain, why I don't know. It's been a busy day, blood taken at 9:40, coffee with Alex, then the support worker from RNID came to help me learn how to put the hearing aid on/in. I think

I know how to do it now. Then I went with a group of others to wrap presents for Santa's Grotto. Came back, made supper and wanted to flake out but couldn't.

So long boring story as to why I'm here writing to you. To tell you how much I miss you. The pain is not so intense now but the longing for you is very strong.

The you that was in our younger years, not the painful times, you needed to leave these behind and have rest. I was thinking of how we met outside college times and rules. Your mother covering up for us, sending me sandwiches because I'd missed supper sneaking out to you, (It was a Christian college of course with 'segregate the sinful sexes' as uppermost.) The daily worry certainly added spice to our romance though.

Just unfortunate that your father was bursar. Remember one night as I leant out of my windows and saw your father coming through the gardens (as a staff member, one of Keith's father's duties was to patrol the grounds periodically). How you scaled a 6ft hedge neither of us ever knew, it was fun. Especially when the dean of women asked what I was doing out of bed that late! 'Going to the toilet.'

Talking with Kathy today and she said a lovely thing about you, 'How many new people coming here will never experience your lovely smile.' So many people say that, 'it's only a smile' but it obviously did a lot of good to a lot of people. Love you lots and I think I'll go to bed now.

November 2009

Nov 6th

As I write this today I can't help thinking of the 5 soldiers killed in Afghanistan. Young men and families and young wives. We were very fortunate that we had a life together and that only age and illness took you away. The figures are nothing compared to the 1st World War. Millions of young men dying, but both then and now, they are all individuals and the pain is still felt by all the families.

This weekend is Armistice Day at the Cenotaph, so minds are turned toward unnecessary death in the pursuit – of what?

Tomorrow night I will watch the Remembrance service from the Albert Hall. That will be the first time in many, many years that we have not watched it together. Another Rubicon to cross for me.

I was thinking of Bala when you marched and participated in the remembrance service with the vicars. Found a picture of that the other day.

Sometimes I think I will list all the things – good or bad – that we have experienced. Just to keep the memories of you and me alive for the family, and our descendants. Glad that you saw and knew our great granddaughter. She'll soon be 4. Again, time takes over all our lives.

Thinking back to our lives, I will try to remember some of our episodes. Not to keep you alive in my mind – I don't need that – but you as an individual, because when I am 'laid in the earth to rest' these memories will be no more. Not that I think they will be in any chronological order, just as I think of them. Love you lots, night.

Remember Togo on our way driving to Ghana on local leave? I was paddling and the undertow pulled me in – if Adrian hadn't noticed and pulled me out, you would have been mourning, not me.

Nov 10th

This weekend I have been utterly lazy. Don't feel well, sore throat, etc., so I, me, who doesn't like TV, have watched and watched it for nearly two days, in between reading the newspaper.

Of course this has been Remembrance time so I watched the Albert Hall and the Cenotaph. Both as always very moving, watching it without you – I thought I would cry but I didn't. I think of all our years and see these young people with children and no partner and I am sorry for us and very sad for them.

Then to go from one extreme to another I watched a Disney film, The Aristocats. Do you remember the lovely jazz scene in there? That's all I watched it for. It was really lovely to hear it.

All I have to look forward to now is an hour's dental work on my back tooth. It has just dropped all the fillings of years, and now needs a crown. You know I've always said I want to die with my own teeth, well I reckon it's cheaper to die!

Do you remember how it took me about six months to get used to kissing you after your false teeth, I really don't like them. We only pecked for a long time. Not good for one's love life?

November 2009

Nov 11th

Today I had to go for results of my blood test. Dr Chris wanted to see me about my thyroid, which is now high as opposed to the last test, which was too low. So, all change.

One good thing came out of this visit to the doctor was that Paul Smith, vicar of Willen, is holding a 6 week course on 'Living with Loss' so I am going to attend this because I feel less anguished but in need of support, I think you would approve.

It's very hard to find words to describe my loss – as different from others – I have a strong faith, so I don't believe that 'this' is the end. But help to cope with the quite natural feelings of loss and loneliness would, I think help me. I do miss you so much.

Have I said before that I didn't like your grave to be untidy -- you know me. I like for you to be taken care of. The trouble of course is that we have to wait for it to settle, it just about has finished now.

But the boys want to do the edging and putting on the chippings, but Julian isn't here until March. In the meantime, you're untidy and I don't like that. Even now I want to take care of you. It's a good job you're 'sleeping'; you'd be worried about me worrying.

It was very interesting at the surgery today. It is Armistice Day and Dr Chris called all the staff and patients to remember the dead for the 2 minutes' silence.

Wasn't that a lovely thing to do, there is a real awareness of what war means in the populace now.

Also, the last chap who remained from the 1st World War died last week. I think people are actually aware of what our freedom now has cost.

As I carry on burbling to you, I must tell you – my tests are good (apart from thyroid) Cholesterol 4.2, and me a chocoholic!, and my blood sugars were 5.0.

It's amazing how that has suddenly made me feel better myself. Now the thing to do, is lose weight.

I caught sight of myself sideways in the wardrobe mirrors, and my face looked so old! I stood there and said 'well darling at least you won't see how I age now. Anyway I think you always saw me as 17. I remember you suggested I wear a dress like the one I wore at 19. Bless your heart, had you forgotten that at the time I was 70. Love you lots.

Nov 15

Hello again sweetheart.

Today I brought you a present, (okay, I know you don't know) but you would like it if you did. It's a lovely Cyclamen with variegated leaves and a white flower whose edges are a lovely deep mauve. Next week I will go to your grave and plant it. Until we (the family) 'do' your grave, as I've said before, the only thing I can do is to at least show we visit you and care enormously.

I've just had a lovely phone call from Hugh, the local Mayor, would I like to go as his guest to the pantomime. I'm very excited. He, like you, likes to shout out, Eileen doesn't "do" panto, so I'm going to be sitting next to a shouter! Who also happens to be the Mayor.

November 2009

You always said you were glad I'm here -- at the village I mean [Lovat Fields Village in Milton Keynes where Liz and Keith lived]; it meant you wouldn't have to worry about me. It's true I am able to participate in whatever I want and this next few weeks for instance I'm going to a function before I go to the 'Dream of Gerontius' [Oratorio by Edward Elgar, 1900 – a favourite of Keith's], then for my birthday I'm going to Falstaff [Opera by Verdi, 1893, based on the comic Shakespeare character]. After that it's the panto. So you were right darling, I am well looked after but I always come back to our apartment and the ache of you not having shared my pleasure is intense.

I love and miss you enormously but it is now a 'toothache' ache, always there but I 'keep taking the medicine.' In other words, I use words out loud and talk to you.

Actually the heart is a tough little thing isn't it, we think its broken but it keeps sending our life-blood round and renewing our life and hope and healing.

Yesterday Adrian and I went out for lunch at a Persian restaurant. The food was lovely, most of the dishes we would and did recognise from eating with Greeks and Lebanese. You would have really loved it.

It's times like this I miss you because I know what enjoyment you would have had, both from the food and being with your sons.

Unfortunately, your last 6-8 years had very little fun and I think we feel the pain very strongly, that we can't do anything to make you happy now.

Please God we all did make you as happy as we could during those bad years.

One day soon, I will write the story of your life, the boys want me to, I don't know why I hesitate but I do.

In the sitting room there's a big box of Thornton's chocolates. I've had them for 24 hours and they are not opened yet, ...a record? But I think I'm just going to weaken.

Remember you had to hide chocolate for me, only to be given when I was desperate? As your illness progressed though, you would forget where you had hidden them, and as you were 6 foot and I'm 5 foot, they were always hidden out of my reach. We've had a lot of fun haven't we. Love you lots.

Something you would like to see now, I have crinkly eyes back again, not because I've lost you but because I sleep now. Today I woke at 9:45 – unheard of – so the 'happy' eyes are returning. I do wish you could see them, it would make you so happy.

Nov 17th

Tonight I went to the 'Living with Loss' meeting 6-8 with the people leading out.

We discussed one of the stages of grief, coping etc. Led by the vicar who visited us when we first moved in, and his wife. It really was enlightening and I found it helpful.

Not that anything can ease the pain of your going. But how to cope that, is something to learn.

Tonight I really miss you, obviously talking tonight has opened wounds, and I'm feeling miserable, low, lost, sad and lonely, need you. Need you to hold me in your arms and say "don't worry, it will be alright." It used to make me so cross. I always said 'how do you know it will be alright?' But it always was! I need that now, tonight, so much.

And I thought I was coping. Managing, doing well, and now I'm crying again.

I keep saying it but I do love you and miss you.

Adrian has just rung to see how the meeting went and of course I've blubbed again. He has and does support me a lot; he and Sue are always there for me.

Do you know what I remembered today? When we drove through Togo and Dahomey and we stopped on the beach for a swim, and I got sucked in by the undertow of the sea. It was Adrian who saw and pulled me out. He says he doesn't remember it. He was only about 14 then.

When I feel like I do now, I want something sweet to eat, and I'm afraid my chocolates have gone. I'm going to rummage around and see if I can find anything before I go to bed.

Night sweetheart, I love you.

Nov 19

Well, today, you have a very clever wife! The two big things I have done today are the sort of situations you would have dealt with – both financial – and you know what finances and me are like.

After 8 months since you died I have eventually got my pension sorted. The DWP have now decided what I am allowed. So as you've always said, "wait till the money's in the bank", but hopefully come next Monday I should know exactly what I have coming in, then I can budget.

Talking of which, son No. 1 rang to say 'they've sold the house' after 3½ years, that is such a relief for them.

Number 2 of my clever clogs act is, I have enquired about insurance for the scooter I've been lent on a long term loan and I have worked it out that putting it on the house insurance is the cheapest way to do it, and I've done it!

I think the girl at the brokers office must think I'm a dummo. Everything she said I stated back in my words and we agreed. I do feel quite pleased with myself, and I think you'd be proud of me.

What I'm trying to do is not lean so heavily on son No. 2. I know he'd willingly do it, but at 77 I should be able to sort these things out. This is one of the disadvantages of our age group. The men 'did' all this sort of arrangement.

So now the populace at large has a non-driver, who's scared of machinery, etc., etc., being let loose. I did make very certain that I have public liability cover. Probably I want so much to go too fast as too slow.

Incidentally the speed range on this scooter has a picture at one side of a tortoise and a hare at the other. Need I say any more about competing with Jensen Button.

Every time I do something like this I always replay in my mind how when you were still able, as to what you would have done. Amazing how much in life we subconsciously absorb. Thanks for all the things I've learnt from you. You've been a good man and I've always respected you as well as loving.

Looking back on these 'ramblings' I don't seem to have told you that for 1 day I was a tour guide. Quite fun.

A group came down – or up – from Birmingham to look round our 'village' before they buy or rent one in Birmingham. What I had to do was to act the part of 'hostess with the mostest', show them around, point out the facilities, answer their questions. I opened our apartment for them to see a real life home, took them to the restaurant for lunch, showed them the classes of line dancing and after everyone had a drink at the bar, they left.

Really I thoroughly enjoyed it, all I needed was a brolly to hold up and keep them together!

They were a lovely group and 2 couples kissed me goodbye, very warm people, all ages from 55 upwards. Again I believe you would have enjoyed seeing me at my best, working with people.

From there I went to the group for communion. We really are catered for here. I am happy as I can be without you, I am happy, and you always said, it made you happy to know I would be safe and have friends in the environment when you died. Rest quietly my love, I am happy.

20th Nov

There was a nature programme on tonight about Black Mambas. Remember the snakes the boys used to catch? This was about Swaziland and a white couple with 3 boys, and the youngest had to do a project and he chose snakes. It sounded so much like our family, but it is the only nature programme that I've watched that has made me cry – with homesickness. I was amazed by my own reactions. We did enjoy our years in Africa though, didn't we?

People still say to me how lovely it was to have Africans singing at your funeral.

You were amazingly well loved you know, in fact just today I had a letter from someone who thanked me for the influence you had on her life. Your life still goes on.

Today we've had 2 of 'our boys' (50+ year olds) here, its nice to see them enjoying each other. No. 3 son we see in March and we try and all go out for a meal together. That will be just a year since you died.

One thinks that you can't go on living yourself after your lover-husband has died, but you choose to live or to die, and to most people, living is what you do.

[Last Week of November, 2009]

The last week has been both busy and hard, joyful and sad. The nice things I have done have been saddened because you would have enjoyed them, and you weren't here. So although enjoying myself in a way, in another, I'm very sad, and missing you dreadfully.

Not being able to share life and thoughts with you makes me aware how lonely I can be.

Yesterday Sue took me to your grave. It was such a sad scene, leaves everywhere, so wet and muddy. I will be glad when we can the grave look better.

Can a grave look better?

November 2009

There is within me a sadness that is different to when you first died.

I love and miss you in so many ways, darling, this time last year you said you didn't think you'd see Christmas; you did, but I now think, looking back, that you wanted to go then.

Still I'm glad that we did decorate for you last year. This year I have no impetus to do anything. I will try to find our crib and 3 wise men. This is what Christmas really means, not a load of frippery. If I'm not careful I shall be Scrooge-ish.

To come to something more positive, the dream of Gerontius was superb, as it was Glyndebourne performing, one would expect it to be. Both the orchestra and the choir were fantastic. You would have loved it. It was a full orchestra; the strings were superb.

And of course we went to the reception first. Probably a hundred people of note and very good light refreshments. Catered for by a firm called 'Red Hat'. I think Sri Lankans. As the reception was in aid of 'Hope Outreach', and Dr Chris's Sri Lankan orphans, it was well attended and a retiring collection was made, and they raised £500. Not a lot, but it will be used well.

The day after that I went to the 'Parkinson's' Christmas Tea. It was held at the garden centre and went well, food was well presented, 86 people present.

The following day I went with Carrie to my 'Christmas present', Falstaff, also performed by the Glyndebourne. Acting really alive and singing tremendous. There was a lot of laughter as the 'Merry Wives of Windsor' led Falstaff a right dance.

As you can see, I am doing things, and you'd love to see me all dolled up. I think you'd think I'd scrubbed up well. My face actually looks better. It's not every night I sleep, but I do get more sleep now, and people keep telling me I'm looking better. It's as well they can't see my heart, that feels cold and sad.

I would love to have your arms around me to cuddle and talk in bed like we used to years ago, before this rotten disease took hold.

I dream of you a lot, sometimes nice, sometimes not.

I pity anyone who suffers from SAD. I personally only need a nice bright sunny day to pick me up.

You now have tête-à-tête snowdrops, primroses, and cyclamen on your grave, and a piece of rock from Cae Du planted there. You are wrapped in my love and care even though everything is horrible there, and me sad without you.

Goodnight my love I'm going to bed again, in the hope that I'll sleep.

December 2009

Dec 3

I've not written for some time because I've not been well. Thought that my shingles was coming back. I felt so lousy and in so much pain.

Well as of today I'm doing something about the pain. I made an appointment to go to the Blackberry Clinic, and I'm paying to go for a fairly long course of treatments for my back and knee.

I wish you could have had this chap, Shai, to help you. When I went, I took my X-rays from NHS appointment where I had been told my hips were all right and not a mention of my lower back or spine.

To save going into boring detail, there is quite a lot wrong, that, taking into account my age, they can help with. The pain has been awful, and you my love suffered so much pain that you would understand when I say I could barely walk.

I have no qualms about getting private treatment for you but I find it hard to warrant spending on me, but I have to. Yes, I'm 77 and I am an old lady but I don't have to walk and move like one.

So here's hoping that a) I'll be able to keep going as long as possible and b) that it works. He said it's a long term job but I should have a lot less pain within 2 weeks.

This coming Monday, Dean is coming to paint the sitting room, then hopefully the carpet will get seen to and I can come, for the first time in $2\frac{1}{2}$ years into our home and not have to live with so much upheaval.

It is still our home, even though it is just me, you are still part of everything I do. I know you would like this that and the other and I talk to you about everything. So much of life has been our life, that I can't see ever changing.

Having emptied the bookcase for the painter I've moved all the CD's, you had so many James Last. I'll play some of them over the weekend and imagine all we've done, where we brought them etc.

Our very first one we bought in Amsterdam, remember? Trumpet Agogo. How sad and lonely not to have memories. When I stand at your grave I do not weep but a great bubble of sadness is within me for, lost memories, lost future. I don't really know how to describe it, just ineffable sadness that you are no longer you, and what we had, has gone.

Little things the boys say reflect the love, honour, and respect they have for you. For me, what were our last years, were filled with just trying to get you better, or at least, a little more comfortable, not living life to the full. Yet, we were together, now nothing except apartness, emptiness.

Still, overall, I think that I have managed and will manage -- one has to, anyway.

Occasionally, I actually laugh, which a while ago didn't seem possible. I even sometimes watch TV. That should make you laugh. Just at the moment I'm watching ballet. Romeo and Juliet with Nureyev and Fontaine. Very old, but wonderful. Remember how you liked Romeo's shirt? And I made you one, I found it the other day.

Sometimes I watch the news and occasionally there's a good documentary. Surprising how the ballet has changed, from this which in its day was the tops, is now quite bland.

Everything is faster now, more aggressive, I suppose this is what life has always been like, appearing to speed up as we grow older. It actually, I think, prepares one for the end of life and thinking it won't be so bad to leave after all.

I'm so glad we were able to nurse you at home. You left one home for another. Unfortunately, not where I can make you comfortable.

As you know darling, I love you very much and hope that I did everything I could for you.

Dec 10

It's some time since I wrote, life seems to have been so busy, which is good, but I fall into bed to tired to do anything. But I do talk to you.

This week I was taken to the Panto as a guest, and when I had finished dressing I looked in the mirror, and said; 'you'd like the look of me tonight darling'.

The thought came into my mind then, that for so long nursing you, I didn't have the time or energy to make the effort of dressing etc. That, I think, was not good for you. I'm sure that although you never said anything, you probably missed seeing me look good. The things we learn too late.

Everything is too late now, but you are always in my thoughts, the times I say 'oh, Keith would like that', so much sharing we take for granted, until it's too late.

Something you would really have enjoyed, was the talk I went to Christopher Martin Jenkins. When I was introduced to him, I said we might have met professionally as you were asked to play for Surrey. He knew Ken Barrington.

The talk was good, anecdotes of various players, he'd even got the accents right of various players. It was very entertaining. Also talked about the future of cricket as a whole and what will happen in the 20/20 [Liz means T20] matches.

I thought of you so much then and how you would have loved it. Adrian came with me and also enjoyed it, but Julian would have loved it. In fact, Julian and CMJ could have been brothers, so much alike in stature and stance.

The past week has for me been very painful, I could hardly walk. In the end I rang up the private clinic to see if they could help. So far I've had 2 sessions and X-rays of my knees. It seems both my knees are very arthritic and I have a cartilage problem in one. My back is already less painful. I can't go for too long because of the cost, but just to have the reason explained and also see the X-rays and where the problem is, makes it easier to do something to help myself.

Helene and I were talking about you the other day (remember the Greek Lady – who, she admitted, was a little in love with you?). I went up to read poetry to her, it transpires that her husband wrote some poetry. Next time I'm taking some of yours up to read to her. She has such fond memories of you.

In many ways (I know it sounds strange) but it's almost as though I know you better after death. Other people's views of you point out some of the things I hadn't seen, too close perhaps. It would be nice to start all over again, but to go on to a happy ending. But one day we'll be together again.

Do you remember when I came home for surgery from Nigeria and Faud [A Lebanese friend in Nigeria] paid for your fare home to be with me? As you came through the door, I literally threw myself at you with surprise and joy. That would be lovely if I could do it now.

Nearly every night I dream of you, sometimes they're nice dreams, sometimes sad, but always your presence is there for me. I love you and miss you so much.

Dec 11

This has been a busy day and I'm very unsettled, don't know why. I'm in pain, that doesn't help, but I miss you. Perhaps its all this building up for Christmas, and last year you said you didn't think you'd last till Christmas. You did, until March.

Alex needed to shop today and so did I; we went by taxi to the centre. Adrian and Sue came this morning. Then a Christmas carol concert tonight. All day busy but nothing to see. Except an aching loneliness for you.

There is no way I would want you back to suffer again, but I am lonely, but I don't think anyone sees it. Hope not, it's a very private grief.

I've been invited to an evening of baroque music tomorrow night in Newport Pagnell. There's so many things that I'd like to do with you, not on my own. Quite a few people here are also very ill, old age mostly, but it makes me sad for them and also myself.

December 2009

Talking to you like this does help. Can't seem to settle into a routine and I'm eating too much. One of the couples here, he is in Willen Hospice, exactly the same as you. I feel so much for them both.

Sorry darling, I'm wittering, but I do so much want the old you, the man I loved, just to cuddle up and go to sleep, sorry darling, goodnight.

Dec 15

The gap in writing is because I've been sick. Not surprisingly in an enclosed building such as this that I've been hatching a cold or something, sore throat, etc., but all I've wanted to do is stay in bed.

Gordon came up yesterday for a few hours while Rosemary had meetings in Watford. It was nice to see him and he took me shopping, all the little bits, Christmas presents, etc. Then we had lunch out and came back and had coffee here at the coffee bar. Talked quite a lot about you and our different ways of missing you, which is interesting, of course our relationship and theirs have been different, apart from being male and female, you've got good sons, and always had their respect. And they are looking after me very well. Although I've said I want to be on my own, they have arranged to check me to see if I'm in need at all.

One of the nice things with Gordon visiting is that hugging and being hugged by Gordon is just like a hug from you, cuddly bear feeling.

Tonight we actually have frosts and possibly snow by the morning, winter is coming with a vengeance now.

The village is beautifully decorated with garlands and trees, it has a lovely family home feel about it. Different to last years coordinated 'corporate' feel. I've had nice cards and thoughts from the Carers – who miss you. So nice that they are thinking of both of us.

Love you lots darling. I really am glad you're at peace and free of pain, but I miss you.

Christmas Eve

Hello my love

' 'Tis the night before Christmas'

Remember reading that to the boys, who now read it to their grandchildren.

The continuity of life is a wonderful thing in its broadest sense isn't it. You are not here now, but you go on through your children, into their children. As I have said when you were alive, something of us as individuals always lives on. This story for instance, and on Christmas morning, before presents, 'The Little Match Girl.'

Tomorrow, Christmas Day, I'm going to read it to Helene, she has never heard it.

Although I'm not 'doing' Christmas, I have been very busy, and now, I am really tired. In fact I'm on my way to bed, but I just wanted to touch base with you, actually I did that this morning. Adrian and Sue took me to the grave so I could have a chat with you.

Your little daffs are coming up as are the snowdrops. The cyclamen I planted a couple of weeks ago are really flowering, although today, under a blanket of snow. Your flowers love you, as do we all.

Being on my own is what I wanted. I just want to think about you and remember our life. Tonight I won't write much because I've actually got an infected foot and it's throbbing. I just want to climb into bed with painkillers and go to sleep.

Goodnight darling.

Christmas Day
Morning darling.

No, it's not happy, for you or me. You are there, thank God with no awareness of my sadness.

I am here with a memory of a dream from last night. You came back to me, and it was wonderful. Only to wake up to 'Merry Christmas' which it isn't. I am not happy without you. This is realistic … 59 Christmases together and now, by my own choice, alone. The boys will ring, but it is you I want.

Every 'anniversary' is just a little easier, but mass happiness is very hard to bear.

My logical mind says I have lots to be thankful for, a lot more than some people, but that doesn't alter the fact that my pain is my pain, and I would do anything to help theirs, but only you could help me.

Still, it's a beautiful day. The sun is just pouring in, and if I didn't have the sore foot, I'd go for a good walk. But all I can bear on my foot is slippers.

After I've visited 2 old ladies on their own here, I will probably sort some drawers out. My mantra, 'do something' I can 'do' while crying, better that way.

I've just finished a book by Laurens Van der Post. Story of a child growing up in Africa. The child was white but had grown up with an African soul. Many times I wanted to cry because of memories there, and the natural way of coping with death and life as well. It was a book that filled my soul not just in a spiritual sense but a full bodied living and coping.

It's the next day now, and I've been on my own all the time and getting 'soggy.' Apart from the fact of looking for something, can't find my sketching bag, it's got all my pens and pencils. I've turned everything out and no joy. I swear I've got gremlins here.

Absolutely NOTHING on TV, but I just caught a trailer of a child's programme, one of those good versus evil ones, genies and dragons, goodies and baddies, it was really good, and I feel better for watching it. Amazing, but I think its just given my mind an escape from reality, and that's what I needed.

Is this 2nd childhood at 77? Possibly as adults we forget the simplicity and faith of children. Anyway I feel better for watching it.

Julian rang yesterday, and they, he and Stefanie, are sad. Eisa, the smaller of the two Labradors is dead, and they really miss her, funnily enough Simba doesn't. Maybe it's because she's now top dog and is enjoying it.

One more day and it's the end of Christmas. I have been lonely and sad, but it's another milestone on my way, and I did the right thing wanting to be on my own, but then I didn't realize that Christmas was 5 days this year. That has been hard. But 1 more day and it's my birthday and the boys will be here. I shall be glad of company then.

You have been in my heart, all the time, and I have cried, but I wouldn't want it any other way. You are at rest, and that's what I wanted for you. I love you lots darling.

Dec 29

Well love, if you were able, you'd remember, it's my birthday today, 77. Where have all those years gone and what have I left in the world? What can I do with what is left.

Such big questions, wish you were here to guide me along the way. It seems as though there's nothing that I can say 'I did that, it helped mankind'. Maybe the boys will come up with some ideas tomorrow, they are here for my birthday.

I go to bed tonight somewhat deflated. I'm just an old woman of 77 and nothing behind or in front of me, Bah humbug!

New Year's Eve

I am now officially 77 (nearly eighty)! The boys gave me a good birthday. We all had lunch in the restaurant, a good meal, good conversation. Our great granddaughter learnt that Mimi doesn't like bad behaviour. Apparently everyone in the restaurant jumped when I told her to sit down. Poor little mite, I did feel sorry for her, but her mother didn't mind, and she now says 'Mimi would not like that, etc., (I am an ogre) actually even the boys jumped. One of the family memories for years to come.

Our biggest memory though was of you and how you would have loved to be at that table with your family. We missed you.

Now New Year's Eve, and life starts all over again. I have no resolutions. (Could do with losing weight though).

But I did something today that I think you would approve of. I have booked a ticket to go to a 'Ball'. In February there is a Mayors Charity Ball, and I'm going as part of a group. I'm really quite scared but also looking forward to it as well.

If you were with me, I would have no qualms, but after 59 years to do this as an individual is scary, but I have to grow, or die.

So my friends here are determined that 'Cinders' shall go to the ball. It is a Caribbean evening, food, steel band, everything.

The general pain of not having you here is a little easier now, I'm adapting, adjusting, whatever, but the 'specifics' to us are very painful and lonely. You will be in my thoughts all the time, 'Keith would have loved this' is what I say an awful lot.

I wish 'Cinders' could go with her 'Prince Charming' of long ago. I've said hello to the new year and looked at a partial eclipse of the moon, it's now time for bed. Night darling.

January 2010

New Year's Day 2010, 8:30 pm

New Year's Day, everything just the same, no earth shattering happenings. No you, just nothing. Can you tell I had a bad night? Lack of sleep is an absolute killer of 'joie de vivre.' Last night I took 2 sleeping tablets, and slept.

Tonight I can't get to sleep. My body clock must be absolutely wrong. Mind you, because I can't sleep I work. The house is looking tidier.

Jan 4

Whatever happened to time, I do not know. I've just been busy all day. I am trying to sort out cupboards, books, etc., the idea is that this will make life easier, ... we'll see.

Last week I gave Charles your lovely pullover I had made for you. Charles and Catia are both really pleased, a little bit more of you whom they love.

Maybe in a week or two I'll have gone through the paperwork and make sure everything is okay, but only with Adrian's supervision. I don't trust myself to know what's important and what isn't. You would have done it had you been here.

Tonight we had snow, in fact the whole country is under snow. This is when I'm so glad to be here, if anything goes wrong, there's always someone to see to it.

I've been going to the private clinic still, hope to be more free of pain as time/money goes on. Today I had a dozen needles stuck into me, acupuncture. I think it has helped, need a bit longer to find out really.

Just off to bed, good night.

January 2010

One of the really good reasons for being here is that I don't have to worry about frozen pipes, etc. If anything the flat gees too hot and I turn the heating down/off, and open windows for a blast of fresh air. I dare not go out, the paths are really icy, but again, apart from unnecessary things I have no need to go out. The temperature is supposedly about -17 tonight. At least it might kill off some bugs in the garden. Again, I am blessed to be here. As you said, you know I'm safe.

This is being written in the middle of the night as pain has woken me up, had drink, tablets, etc., but can't get back to sleep.

The thought of you lying in a cold snowy bed makes me sad, but my sense and faith, knows you're not there, but I feel for you. But nothing to the sadness and frustration of you being in so much pain and I couldn't help.

Darling, I don't cry so much now, 'It', the pain, sadness, whatever, has become more manageable, but oh I do miss you so much. On the outside I imagine people think I'm better, none of us knows another's emptiness.

There isn't much point without you. Even one day is a long time. Yes, I keep busy, but that's all it is, busyness, not anything with a purpose for the future, especially hard when the night is longer than the day. Yet we have the tidiest linen cupboard since we've been here!

I've sorted stuff out and its gone to various charities and people so nothing is wasted. All I need now is just a change for my bed and towels. I've brought a really good blow-up bed if the boys come, so I've kept linen for that, so, tidy cupboard.

The next thing I tackle will be all the drawers, papers, etc., so by the time I've finished, I won't have any work to do.

I shall go and make a cuppa now, and then try to go back to bed and sleep. If you were awake now, you'd be asking for a peanut butter sandwich, which I hated the smell of. Me, I want chocolate, but I'll settle for tea and a ginger biscuit.

Love you lots darling, sleep well.

Jan 8th

We really are in the middle of a 'big freeze' as it's called. Remember the year my mother came for a week and couldn't go for 6 weeks? I think it didn't really melt until March.

My only hope is that we (as in the nation), learn how to cope with this weather better.

4,000 schools closed. In our day you just went. More than anything now it seems to be "Elf and safety' the darlings might fall over. We constantly fell over, because we made slides.

Ah well, not a good day anyway for me, I don't like being confined to barracks, but to even go into our garden would be foolish at the ripe old age of 77. Mind you, it would probably be the quickest way to get my knees done, but I'll let discretion rule.

I have to open the doors and windows though, must have fresh air. A 10-minute blast and then close up. Scotland had -20. I am glad to be here, the only problem I have is I can't get to put the rubbish out.

January 2010

Jan 9th

The whole country is now snowbound. I went outside onto our terrace and walked a few steps towards the main building, 1st time in 10 days! While I like the knowledge that someone else deals with all the maintenance etc., I really do feel penned in.

Just watched the news and an elderly couple have been found dead in their bungalow, after having asked for help from Age Concern, Social Services, etc., and this is a civilised country. I'm angry for them but it does underline that we did the right thing to move into a retirement village. As you said, you knew I would be safe.

When I think of you darling, I choke up very easily, I think I miss you more than I acknowledge really. You've been beside me for nearly 60 years, how can I not feel the loss of half myself. I love you and miss you so much. I wish we were together again.

It's such a long time since the real you was around, and of course it has been years – oh darling do you remember how I liked that song that Kathleen Ferrier sang "What is life to me without you? What is life now you are dead?" I have liked it for nearly 50 years, but never ever thought I would feel it in my inner being.

January 12th

Last night and today have been hard, I miss you and there is no love, nothing but emptiness. The weather is appalling and I physically hurt as well as my heart and my inner being.

January 2010

I got to thinking, had I done enough for you. I've been this way before and I thought I had jumped that hurdle, but back it comes again. I'm just so glad death is a sleep, you know nothing of my pain and distress.

But as is usual for me I got on and did something. While thinking and praying, in my nightie I came across some of your artwork, cards, etc., that you were one day going to copy. This was my answer to prayer, your voice telling me everything is okay. In 3 of them you tell me how much you love me and always will, that I've been a good mother to our 3 sons and how you love me more than you did in 1953. I needed that today. Now I just want to go and cry myself to sleep. I do so love you.

This is the day I've been for treatment. I hurt less than when I went in but of course, new parts hurt because of the treatment. I wish I had started this 2-3 years ago, but it wouldn't have done much good, with lifting you so much.

Michael had to go to the hospital today and as yet, 6 hours later, I haven't heard from Alex. I do hope she rings soon.

Reading these words from you with your lovely handwriting has been so good for me today, I can hear you saying the words. Night darling. Every morning when I get up I always hesitate to put the light on, in case I wake you, conditioning I suppose. I always look to make sure, it feels as if you're there, but it's only 'Fred' the teddy bear.

January 2010

Jan 14th

We still have snow, nearly 3 weeks now, but today it is starting to melt, but still a bit icy underfoot… . So I have had no chance to even start looking for a 'ball gown', only 3 weeks to go until the charity ball and I quite literally have nothing to wear.

Probably the last time I wore a 'posh frock' was in Africa at one of the banquets. Tomorrow I may be able to get to the city centre and see if there is anything in the sales. If I had thought, or known before Christmas I might have had some luck. Anyway, tomorrow I'll see what I can find.

Jan 19th Tuesday

This week is a hard week again. I miss you so much, and just today I've had Alex down here. Dr Chris has just been to them and said, what I have seen (and it makes you come to mind), that Michael is dying. It is so hard for her because she doesn't have the family support that we do.

I also think Michael needs to be told. You knew and had made yourself ready, that is better for the sick one I think. My heart aches for them and also for myself and you.

The pain doesn't get less, just able most times to handle it. Not today.

Compounded by the fact that Helene died last night, and Harry from the Parkinson's group died of a heart attack last night.

Normally I'd run into your arms, but now I can't and I miss you and love you and you're not here.

January 2010

How does one describe this? It feels like pain --
as in it hurts -- but it also feels numb, you don't
hurt because you can't feel, then again it's like
something has punched you in the gut, but you
feel nothing, the reality of you dying does hurt so
much.

I thought I was managing so well. Why I think
I should cope better than the others I don't know.
All I can say is, I love you, I love you, I love you.

Helene's funeral is on Saturday, Carrie is taking
me and Adrian. It will be at the Greek Orthodox,
then to the Crematorium, then back to Eileen and
Hugh's. I will only go to the funeral.

It's Alex's birthday so after the funeral I go to
lunch with them.

Next week will be Harry's funeral. Maybe
February will bring some joy.

Although I'm sounding, and am sad, my life in
general is growing. I am coping, I am stepping out
of my comfort circle quite often.

I want to do some writing about Africa. The
desk is clear. Adrian has shown me how to do
things on the computer, but just now my heart is
too heavy.

Tonight I watched a programme on the 'Rift
Valley.' It was lovely, so many animals we'd either
seen or had as pets, including a tree Hyrax like
Paddington. [Liz is referring to a pet we had in
Liberia; he was about the size of a small rabbit, and
looked so remarkably like Paddington Bear that we
called him that.] It was lovely to hear that little
'tweety' sound. Right now I can see our
Paddington scurrying in a hurry across the floor

and climbing up the leg of the bed to nestle in the hollow of my neck.

We've had a lot of fun haven't we, will there be any more? I do hope so, but I haven't seen it yet.

January 29

Catkins are out, bulbs are sprouting and grass is pushing up so spring is coming. It might be only a hint, but that is enough for us to have hope of light and warmth.

Almost a year since you died, it doesn't seem that long to me, but it does to my 'heart.' That nebulous organ that we think is the repository for our feelings. Ah well.

Today I went to the Dr's, can't walk properly, and my thyroid isn't working properly, so all in all I feel lousy. 2 appointments at the hospital in February and March. Another MOT, one day I'll be in full running order.

January 30

Darling,

Today I went to Helene's funeral at the Greek Orthodox Church. Remember I went for the Easter service last year? Their very first service. It has now been refurbished and it looks really good, with a lot of icons, and of course there will be more.

As I expected the service was in Greek, part chanting, part spoken. It was very beautiful.

Carrie took me and we both had to get back, me to Alex's birthday and Carrie to her job, so we didn't go back to the house for lunch.

The eulogy was given by her son and was quite deep and full of feeling and respect. From this I learnt quite a lot about Greek history and also a lot about Helene.

Later on Julian and I spoke about some words and their meaning then and now, from the Greek language. I didn't realize how little I know of Greek history, both ancient and modern. Also how much Greek there is in our own language. Learning is so stimulating.

Night darling.

February 2nd

Soon it will be a year since you died, so long ago. One certainly doesn't 'get over it.'

Today, for instance it's as raw as ever, I'm lonely, and that means 'alone' as in there is only part of the whole here, me.

There's people everywhere and today I've had the job of showing people round the complex, so I've been part of quite a large group, and yet, and yet, I am alone, that means right now, without you.

I do love you darling, and miss you, so much. I don't know what to do with what is left of my life, my physical life that is. The rest of me is with you.

Yesterday Adrian and I bought all the stuff for the boys to do the grave. Not that you'll know anything about it, but you will be tidy. It matters to me that I look after you, I did in life, I will do it in death as usual. I've got a super picture of you on the desk, with your crooked smile, it makes me feel closer to you.

As you can see from today's writing, I'm sad, and really all I can do is to work through this, no tablets to kill the pain, however I do eat a lot of chocolate, that helps, not my weight though.

One thing I did today, just for myself, I brought flowers. Yellow tulips and lilies, (don't think I've ever seen yellow ones before) and carnations. The lovely soft yellow tulips are next to your photos and the others are in the sitting room. I really get pleasure from fresh flowers in the house. My extravagance for the day. But it looks good.

Tell you what was nice today was mixing here with young people. The group were from 25-35.

So used to being with older people I didn't realise I missed the other age group, but as you and I have always worked with and for younger people, I shouldn't be surprised that today gave me pleasure.

Love you lots darling, 'night.

February 5th

Yesterday was a busy day, and part of today has been busy and tomorrow I'm going to be Cinderella, wish you were coming as my prince.

But, as I have said before, I have to take the big step and try to enlarge my life, to live without you and not just to exist.

Today is Friday and yesterday was Michael and Alex's Diamond Wedding Anniversary, we just missed it, didn't we? They had a card from the Queen (I thought it was a photocopy) and then nearly spilt coffee on it!

But for all the problems surrounding the day, they enjoyed their day.

Tuesday I took a group round the complex. Wednesday at my art class (breakthrough there, I can actually see a line to start from), difficult to explain, but my problem has been I don't know where to start. This week I did, and the girl who takes our class said I obviously see lines of a drawing as Picasso did.

Wouldn't it be ironic if of all the beautiful representative art I enjoy, I turned into a Picasso that I can't stand. Anyway I'm quite excited by my small progress.

Today I went to look for strappy sandal shoes to go with my long dress for the ball and by chance saw Adrian and Sue in Stony as Carrie had driven me to Stony. We had planned to have lunch, so 4 of us went to the Thai restaurant. Nice time, especially as it is Sue's birthday.

Another useless piece of information, I'm hobbling around almost unable to put my heel to the floor, unbearably painful, but on trying on my 'glass slippers' I bought today to go with my 'ball dress', and walking around to see if they are right with my dress, I can walk better!

It seems that my weight is forward enough, no pressure on my heel. Can't ponce around in silver high heeled slippers every day though. Will have to buy some shoes with heels rather than flat, what a shame!!!

Adrian has given me his granddad chair, would have been ideal for you, but although it's very big, it's very comfortable for me.

I'm now off to bed, to get my beauty sleep for tomorrow, love you lots.

Feb 6th

I am nervous darling.

Tonight I'm going to be all dressed up and gay to a large crowd of people (which I really have always found hard) and I don't have you by my side, you always boosted my confidence and you weren't good at small talk in groups, we matched each other and now I'm on my own and scared. The fact that friends are looking out for me is wonderful, but I want you, oh dear, I must not cry.

Really I set myself this test, but I wish I hadn't.

Julian has just said he'll ring me tomorrow for a blow by blow account. Theirs a thought, if he wasn't in Germany he could have taken me.

February 2010

Of all the boys, he would be most comfortable in this situation. He's just told me I've got to dance, even if the only dance I ever learned as a youngster was to jitterbug!

Writing to you is the next best thing to talking, in my mind after 59 years I know the sort of thing you'd say to me. I'm incredibly grateful for all these years, life had a purpose and a reason.

Even at the end there was a purpose, keeping you comfortable and free from pain.

Now it's just making sure the house is clean and I eat, Boring!

Anyway, I must say to myself, tonight is a BIG step, so long as I don't fall over in my 'dancing shoes.' Just going to the hairdressers, talk soon.

Past midnight and I'm in bed so writing is worse than usual.

Carrie came and made me get ready to go, I really wanted to back out, my dress wasn't right, cleavage too low, I was overdressed, etc., etc. But once I got there, I knew I was alright.

You would have liked the way I looked tonight. Life goes by too quickly, you and I didn't do enough 'going out.'

The evening was good, a very good menu including rice and peas and jollof rice, the steel band was a lovely background. There were a lot of people there. I do hope they raised a lot of money for the orphanage.

I won a bottle of good white wine, I think it's good anyway. Probably open it when we are all together in a couple of weeks.

February 2010

My last big step without you I think, I wore the jewellery you brought me a couple of years ago, it matched my dress beautifully. Thank you.

Monday 8th Feb

Well Cinderella has had her ball, and nothing has changed except I've got over another hurdle and learnt to wear high heels again, the heel takes the pressure off my heel so I am walking more on my toes.

Sometimes when I write to you I feel as though I need to go and post the letter, and just now I was going to say, 'I'll send you a photo of how I looked that night. Silly girl, but I know I looked good, and the lovely necklace and earrings you bought me just brought out the colour of the dress. In fact I think it's probably 20 years since I wore earrings.

It's just a month now and you will have been dead 1 year. That word dead; is a horrible word, it means to me at least, the cessation of you as a person, and you haven't ceased.

This past week I have missed you so much, in bed, walking, talking, listening to music, looking at art, all things where I want to say 'oh look.' I do say that, and then grizzle because I know you are not there, but you are in my inner being.

I cuddle Fred, the teddy bear, a lot at night, poor thing. I grizzle at him, squeeze him tight, lift him up by his tail, and in the morning he is usually on the floor, but he is very cuddly. I call him 'Fred the Ted.' You know how much I hated the name Fred.

Sometimes the tears do overwhelm me, I think it's because they come so unexpectedly.

February 2010

A nice thing has just this minute happened to me. Remember I said I'd shown some people round the complex? They've just bought me a lovely bunch of flowers to say thank you. A nice group of youngsters. I'm still searching for a role in life. Working with people is what I can do I know, but where or what, I wait and pray.

12th Feb

Last date I wrote was on the 8th. Somehow these last few weeks have been harder than just after you died. I miss you so much, achingly so. I think I really begin to understand 'bereft.' Half of me has gone and I will never be whole again.

At the moment it is too raw to even go to your grave. Probably the winter months don't help, but I suppose no time is right in that sense.

Carrie and I went to the Persian restaurant for lunch today, 'ladies who lunch.' It was her 65th birthday. It was a lovely meal, and she's good company.

I went to do a little 'nuts and seeds' shopping and I realized what a short fuse I'm on, the assistant just talked and talked and said nothing. I do not want to become a cantankerous old biddy; but I feel it coming on.

As I have said before in these letters though, if you had been left behind it would have been worse for you, whatever happens, women as a general rule cope better. We still have a house to run, and if you have children, it must in one way be much worse, but in another it keeps you ever busier.

The coming week is the last but one of the meetings 'living with loss'. The title of the meeting is, 'what next?' If there is an answer to this I would be very happy because at this stage I don't see a next, just another day. The time is 11:30 and I came to bed because I was so tired, but, no sleep.

Oh what a gay life I lead, next week, orthopaedics for knee; 3 weeks later endometriologist to try to balance my thyroid. Then I need cataracts done, by 2011 I shall start off as a new model.

Bulbs are poking through all over, including the snowdrops on your grave. Some days you can feel spring. I am so looking forward to being able to potter in the garden. That always makes me feel better, but apart from that, new life, new hope, somewhere, all these things help the coping process, its been such a cold winter.

Well darling, I will try again to sleep, goodnight, God bless and keep you.

P.S. I've come to the end of this book. I have to start another one. Maybe tomorrow, but over the weekend sometime.

Do you remember you used to write some lovely letters when you were away? I truly don't think I realized how much you loved me, certainly as I have said to you many times, that I love you with all I have and am, but I believe your love was bigger.

My childhood I've tried to forget and not wallow but, it has had an effect on all my life. I still love you with all I have, and thank you for the deep love you had for me.

Love you, night.

I don't mind solitude and aloneness, but not emptiness, solitude for me must produce … what? but something more than nothingness.

Feb 13th
Hello darling,

Sitting here at the desk in the study with a Brahms Violin Concerto playing and it has been a sunny day, cold but sunny, and today I'm feeling a little better, emotionally as well as reduced pain in my foot, lousy night, but the day is better.

I'm reading another book of Henri Nouwen's about the Desert Fathers and solitude and it occurred to me that to some degree the 'empty half' person I feel means I can retreat into my own private desert, through solitude here at our own home.

I do wish I could really talk to you. I think towards the end you must have entered – this place of solitude. Just you and God together. This would explain your peaceful acceptance of the end, in other words it's what you wanted, longed for, a real union with God.

This is also what I long for, but I have to work it through on a different level to you. Love you lots.

Feb 14th
Valentine's Day without you.

This music is beautiful, better on the Bose player in here though, this player is good for light music.

February 2010

There was a programme on TV, about Indian railways. Mumbai. It was so interesting, but it so reminded me of Africa. Noise, lots of it, masses of people, colour, I could almost smell it. It was wonderful.

I so wish that memories could be shown like slides onto a screen and we could really see the past again. Another thing I watched was the 1st of a series on diplomacy through our embassies. Something was said that we have often talked about.

We don't appear to have proper diplomats now, just politicians. Diplomacy is something that one has to feel and know in your innermost being, not sound bites.

Yet another subject we could talk over.

Miss you.

Feb 16

Tonight I went to the last but one of the 'Living with Loss' programme. The last one is a social evening.

It has been quite good but for me I'm not sure what it has done, maybe it will help as I go forward and things will fall into place. It has been very good of Sue to take us, 'us' being another resident here whose husband died 2-3 years ago, and me.

Today was 'what next' but we didn't really touch on that. I did learn one thing though. There is a group called 'Cruse' for widows. I might just look that up.

One thing Paul said tonight was about a journey in solitude. That strikes a chord for me, Henri Nouwen and the Desert Fathers. I think this is my desert, getting from one side to the other, ploughing through sand and dunes, to find, not THE ANSWER, but my answer, to this situation, and hopefully a way to the other side and a deeper understanding of life in relationship to myself.

The vicar's wife, who is a bereavement counsellor, said why didn't I give her a ring. I might.

OK, wash, brush teeth, and hopefully sleep. Last night I was awake until 3:00am. Goodnight, love you.

Feb 19

Today I played a recording of the BBC programme Silverville that we were in.

Watching, I felt quite detached and it seems so wrong to say I'm glad you died, but no one would want to see you suffering like that for much longer.

All I can think is, it doesn't matter how I feel or the loneliness I live with. You are at peace, and I remember so well you telling me 'I've made my peace with God, I'm ready to go'. It was another 5 months before you found that peace, and I can only say I am glad for you.

On this DVD though, it was good to see your lovely smile again. I loved you so much – and still do in a quiet and peaceful way. Now I think I begin to understand what it means to be at peace.

The sun has been shining all day and what a difference that makes to al our outlooks, everyone looks happier, smiles more. It's been a super day, I've even polished the furniture, that also looks nice, it feels like our home.

Everything I do; the thought comes to mind – '… think Keith would like this.' Right now I'm sitting in what was my bedroom when you were sick. It is now the study, and at a real push I can make it a dining room, but for now it's a study. There's a small armchair by the window and I can look out onto the gardens and bowling green. I've got music on, and, like you, I am at peace.

More yesterday and today than I have been before. I feel blessed to have some calm in my life and I feel very close to you, and I have to keep repeating, I love you.

This is the start of the weekend, and hopefully I will find it also peaceful. Next weekend the boys will be here. It will be lovely but not peaceful and calm!

Feb 22

This has been a horrible weekend. I've lost my golden wedding ring you brought me. I've hunted everywhere; emptied all rubbish bins, and gone through them, did some polishing so I've looked in the polish tins, in rubber gloves, shaken all duvets, stripped bed, shaken pillows, under the bed, down the side of chairs, emptied cupboards and drawers, checked coat pockets, just everything I can think of and cannot find it.

My heart is aching with the pain of missing you and now another piece of you has been sliced off me, it was the Welsh Gold one you brought me for our golden wedding. Very special, and I'm sad for you, I don't have your love, and now I don't have your ring either.

Tomorrow the boys come and the weather doesn't look good at all for doing your grave. Adrian tells me not to worry, it will be done. He gave me such a big hug today, it really helped. I've just had a glass of 'Black Mountain', Gwyn's present to me. We've had it before, it is a good tonic – and please may it make me sleep.

Tuesday 23rd

Well, yes, it did make me sleep but I could sleep all today as well. Not a good idea at all.

Julian and Stefanie are driving over from Germany today, and it's snowing. I will be glad to hear from them tomorrow. This has been a very long and cold winter, hope spring comes soon. Everyone is cast down.

Found it darling, in a corner of the bathroom floor, how it got there I just don't know, just saw it from the toilet. I am so happy, I have a piece of you back again, my prayers have been answered.

Saturday 27th Feb

Well darling, although I haven't seen the grave, it is done. The boys have 'put you to bed' and they say it looks better. I will go next week. Even without seeing it I personally feel better, you've been looked after, not thrown aside and forgotten.

To have all three boys together is rare, so that was nice for me, and I believe good for them. They worked for 2 days in rain and cold winds, but it is done. We all went to the Persian restaurant for lunch, again a togetherness time, plus of course the good food we all like.

February 2010

Julian and Stefanie left this morning to go to Aberdeen. He's lecturing there for a month. We discussed his lectures yesterday as a family, we all wish we could hear them when given.

I'm so fortunate with my daughters-in-law. Stefanie and I are really getting on really well together, especially as we see each other more. We as a family have been enormously blessed, but with that comes our responsibilities to others and I believe that as a family we have 'passed it on'.

Now everyone has gone and I am left with the clearing up. I don't mind but it's a lovely day and I might even do some gardening.

And I did, spent about an hour out there, moving and tidying, it felt like spring and I wanted to dig and plant. The sun shone, and it was really quite hot. Now, it's raining again, but at least the terrace looks tidier and I have planted the snowdrops from your grave.

Love you darling, and I feel better now you're tidier, not that I've seen it yet. Hope I approve.

March 2nd

Did I say that Stefanie feels she has a home to go to, (ours) as her Mother is dead and Dad has a new partner? Again and again I say, we are blessed no end with our family.

Not much money between any of us, but we have a strong bond of caring. The boys are all over 50, they feel good about having 'put you to bed', the last thing they could do for you.

Julian has started his lectures in Aberdeen. We might see them again in the summer, which will be nice.

Today I think I've made a mistake. I let the hairdresser put blond mousse on my hair. I look like Maggie Thatcher, brassy blond. Don't like it but it will wash out. After all the work on your grave in the wind and rain, Adrian is sick and so is Gordon. Poor lads can't settle to sleep. Not exactly worried about money, but there isn't quite enough to replace things as they go, but somehow I do manage.

I need a comfortable recliner for me, carpets replaced and some upholstery done. Maybe little by little. Off to bed love, goodnight.

Wednesday 3rd March

More info from DWP, so I've been sitting here trying to work it out. I don't waste money but it just goes. Today I sinned, I have ordered a book from Bibliophile, on art.

Talking of art, I wish we could go up to London. There is a display at the British Museum of the Ife Heads from Benin in Nigeria. It would be wonderful to see them as we had seen some of them at Ife itself. Wasn't it at the Oni of Ife's palace we were spoken about on the talking drums. Tonal drums and our own tonal drums – a great experience.

That was last night, today has been quite good. I actually feel almost human. There are days when I'm covered with a thick blanket of heaviness and occasionally now, a day of enlightenment. Today was one such.

It is bitterly cold but bright and sunny and today I've sorted out some of the 'bothers' or at least have been able to put them on the back burner, so tonight I go out to the 'girls' evening and then to bed and read, and if I'm lucky another good night's sleep. And so, one day at a time.

I love you and miss you lots, but you'd be proud of me. I'm managing and you know how I get in muddles, but I'm OK. Night.

March 5

Darling I wish I could tell you about today. I feel so close to you and grateful for having a faith. Today out of the blue good things have happened. Firstly, I had an appointment booked for someone to come and discuss getting a recliner chair for me, and I made him coffee. He meanwhile was looking (as I would) at our bookcases. He said "That's an interesting title 'Christianity is Jewish' by Edith Schaeffer …" so we talked about the title and he said he was Jewish so I said so were you. We talked for over 2 hours. It was interesting to meet someone who knew something about life, etc. A man of 65 so he had done some living. As he was leaving he said "has anyone said the Kaddish for your husband?" (Remember? The prayer for the dead.)

It was something I didn't think about when you died, so the answer was no. He said he would say it tonight (Friday) at the synagogue for you if I liked! I was completely overwhelmed.

Last week the boys had 'put Dad to bed' (did your grave), and now, through 'the kindness of strangers' the Jewish prayer of mourning was being said for you. It feels so right, and if you were aware I know it would have touched you deeply.

I'm so pleased that the final act is being done for you, and today I saw the grave, you do look nice and tidy and loved and now the Kaddish and after that on Sunday the memorial service at the city church from the hospice for all who have died this year.

Then 2 weeks later will be the first anniversary of your death. I would miss you even if it was the 21st, but your worrying about whether your life has been lived for others, if you only knew the respect and love you left behind your worries would have disappeared. Certainly today has been full of emotion and thoughtfulness for me.

Until tonight when Alex rang.

Michael collapsed on the floor and had – rather unwillingly – to be taken to the hospital. Alex is staying the night with him. I pray for them both, a good couple and their support for me when you were dying was absolute.

Darling, I feel today you have been utterly loved and tucked up in bed, in God's arms, rest in peace my love, goodnight.

Sunday 7th March

Darling,

Just off to the memorial service for those from the hospice who have died this year, you are one of them, and your name will be read out.

My stomach is churning as if I am going through the funeral again. I imagine most of the people attending feel the same. I don't like the term closure, it sounds too American, but I suppose really that's what the effect can be for some people. For me and the family it is another process. Almost you have been 'laid to rest' in a way that mirrors your life.

All parts of your living have been touched on by your dying. Just this last week.

The boys 'put you to bed', I've visited your grave, we are in the process of choosing and organising your grave-plate, the Kaddish has been said or you, now a memorial and then in 13 days' time it will be a whole year since you died.

Those words, dead, died, somehow don't explain or mean anything except you are no longer with me in whatever state of illness.

I am alone, it is that simple. Alone. Bereft. I love you darling, talk to you when I get back. ……

I'm back.

At your funeral and your wake I didn't cry, but today to try and sing The Lord's My Shepherd just broke me. Again, to say 'I miss you so much', is just an understatement. Some deep part of me (my heart?), has been split. I'm no longer whole, just a part after 59 years.

Sara held me while I cried, as a child we were not close, but as a woman, we are, maybe because she herself is now a mother. I decided that we all needed not to come straight home, so we went out for a meal. It was good that we did that, it cooled the emotions, now I'm going to bed, please God to sleep, and not to think of you tonight.

Love you.

14th March

This week I haven't been able to write, although I have said a lot to you. It's really difficult this week, I feel as though I'm in no man's land. Partly this is because I'm still in pain in my legs and feet, walking is difficult, but sitting doing nothing is also difficult.

Then of course this week will be a year since you died. A year since we were last together. In reality I had lost you a long time ago, but you were still here. I'm sure I didn't know how much I loved you, until I had time and rest on my side.

Really I must have worked on remote control for these last few years, and most certainly in the last few months. You know how much I loved you though. I only pray that nothing I said or did made the going harder. I do wish we had our time together again, but without your pain and distress.

Really don't know why I feel as bad as I do, I'm lonely sad and directionless. What to do, and of course I can't walk properly. I do love you darling.

Yesterday Adrian and Sue took me out because I was so low, that was very thoughtful of them. We went out to the Emmaus village, a project run to help those less fortunate than we are. There's books, bric-a-brac, clothes, etc., and on the way there we saw masses of snowdrops. I thought how you would love to see them.

We stopped at your grave and I had potted up some snowdrops and primroses for you.

Today was Mother's Day, and the boys rang and Adrian and Sue and I went out to lunch. Oh, darling, everything is so empty without you. They also took me to the 'Cathedral of trees', remember?

Today was bright and cheerful and there were lots of snowdrops and daffs will be out in a few weeks. All lovely to look at and setting me off on remembering when we saw it.

I don't suppose there will be a time when I don't say 'wish Keith was here'. Goodnight darling.

17th March

St Patrick's Day, leprechauns stuck on windows, people with silly hats on and Irish music all day. Irish music I love, but this is all OTT. I'm not even sure we've got more than one person living here who is Irish.

It's not a good day, been to the optician and today I understand your problem when they put drops in your eyes. Not only can you not see properly but it makes you a bit sick as well.

Anyway, I've put off having my cataracts done for 2 years or more so now I've started the proceedings. Yesterday was my ears, Monday and Wednesday eyes, Thursday exercises for my leg, Oh joy and delight, I'm falling apart, but unlike you darling, I'm not suffering, just angry at age I think, which is silly but c'est la vie.

On a more cheerful note, I saw my first primroses yesterday. Can't remember ever being so glad to see spring, the daffs have dropped their heads and are showing yellow. Lovely.

19th March

Last March at this time you were very ill, dying, retreating into yourself, no talking, just like a little bird, opening your mouth for the crushed ice I had done for you on a piece of gauze. I do wish I had thought to do more for you. Your legs pained, I rubbed them for you with lavender oil, trying to ease the pain and relax your body.

We knew you were dying and so did you, but you were ready to go and go you did, peacefully with all the boys in some way touching you, telling you how much they loved you, I was rubbing your legs and saying I love you, and from that evening into the night you were slowly leaving us.

The boys had made me go to bed and promised to wake me. I needed some sleep and you were safe. Julian woke me, come now Mother, and an hour or two later you died, very peacefully, with no pain because the nurses had syringe drivers working all the time with morphine and a relaxant.

This night a year ago at 3:00 in the night, when the soul often leaves the body.

You did go in peace darling. Everything that could be done had been done for you.

The Ghanaian doctor who came next morning to see to things, was pleased to see the family there with their father. He said it was like his home, it made him happy.

I am going to light the candle that came from the memorial service when I go to bed, and it will burn to the end.

March 2010

Of course I'm sad and weeping, but I love you, loved the person you were and now I'm empty, just still coping. So long as my leg continues to improve I will make some sort of life, writing probably. Don't need new legs for that.

Karyn Till told Adrian, 'your Dad was an unsung hero'. She was very fond of you.

I'm going to bed now, and will think of you and pray for when we meet again.

I love you, I love you, I love you. Good night darling.

4:30 am: Just woke up. By this time last year you had been dead for 1 ½ hours. I was still going in and out of the room telling you I loved you, and now, I have survived my first year without you, as one does. Probably from here, life will be a little easier. I know that I can go on without you, I can go on with loneliness and sadness but always going on. There are others who cannot.

I'm older, we've lived our life and have a belief that we shall be together again. Some of those army wives who have lost their loves and have young children. Their pain must be very hard to bear.

I lit a candle for you last night, and went to sleep. Now, can I still carry our love and past, but go really forward? I need a future, so I must go and find it, and one day maybe I will cry all these tears that still haven't purged me of my sorrow. Love you lots and lots.

What really frightens me is that I have no idea who or what I am, what do I do? I seem an absolute nothing, just an old lady getting older and more decrepit. I don't think I realised that when you died you would take me with you.

I know what I want to say but none of it comes out properly. Just a being who had another half of herself, and now that is not so.

March 22

Jeanette came today, I think I did talk about her. She's a bereavement counsellor, but also a friend. I thought this was a one-off visit to just help me along, but no, she wants to see me again, and do you know, I think she will help me, help me back on track so to speak.

She asked searching questions, which I have to answer to myself. You would like her, she is leading me to see and do what is right for me. Leading, as you always said from your Relate training, not telling.

I hope I can grow, this new prison is getting me down. Darling, as I look at photos of us, (I was tonight, while looking for something else) we have certainly seen a lived life, apart from your departure. Part of me is no longer there or functioning. This whole weekend has been the most tearful of the whole year.

I know what you would have said, 'don't worry, it'll be alright'. Of course the annoying thing was, it usually was alright.

Have I said before that I sometimes feel like Munch's Scream, well I do, the whole face is contorted with fear, dread, disintegration (that's how I saw it). I haven't looked in a mirror, (well neither have I screamed) while screaming, but the picture evokes my feelings.

I understand that the picture was the way Munch felt, as though his world, his society was going into oblivion. Yes, that's about right for me too.

I loved and I do love you darling and I wish I could go to bed and cuddle up and all would be right with the world. Goodnight sweetheart. Now there's a word not used much now. Must look it up sometime, and the word 'partner'. See, writing to you actually makes me feel better, as though you are really listening.

March 27

It is now one year and one week since you died, and everything has gone on just as before, except inside me. My heart, my being, my soul, somewhere inside there's a void. But its true one does go on, what else can you do, lie down and die yourself?

Yes I miss you but I do go on, and you who knew me so well will understand that with spring coming that means I can go into the garden. Not that we now do have a 'garden', just a terrace, but even so, that's enough now.

Yesterday I went to a garden show at the centre. And at long last I have suddenly found what our garden needs. It is an iron open work table and chairs, etc. The wooden pieces were too heavy for a terrace. Suddenly everything has clicked and I think this year will be just what I want. Also I think it's what you would like as well.

Writing to you like this does make me think I will get an answer, and I was going to say 'I'll send you a picture of the garden'. It feels that close.

March 2010

This weekend Julian and Stefanie are here on their way back to Germany, they'll be staying the night and driving down to Dover the next day after we've had lunch at the Persian restaurant.

The weather forecast for next week is snow. Heigh Ho for the garden. Still spring will come. From the beginning of time the seasons have come one after the other. So be it.

I'm sitting up in bed writing this, and wondering will I always write to you. I think I will, but maybe not so often. There is no way I want to ever not be a part of you, after 59 years together, how can all of that living stop.

I do wish we could talk together, cuddling up in bed and putting the world to rights was so good. We used to have some good conversations, didn't we? I miss your mind as much as your body.

That actually was the hardest part of your illness, seeing you disappear, as in the mind, the essential you was gone, wish I could tell you now how much I loved you.

We had bad times, everyone does, but always came through the stronger, both in ourselves and our relationship with God.

I'm glad you told me, you didn't think you'd live much longer, but you had made your peace with God. From then on, you were waiting to go. We all miss you so much, but you are at peace.

Julian and Stefanie will be here this evening, in time for a late supper. Today is Stefanie's birthday, so I've got a special little cake for her. This will probably be the last time I see them for about a year, so its rather nice to get together again.

March 2010

There are many reasons why I wish you were here with me. Now, it's because I hear a bird I can't identify, and you were always so good at bird sounds. The sound is as if the bird was hitting metal, a chink, chink. Difficult to see because it was against the light, but small. I think it was a stonechat, no one seems to know. So you see, I miss you for many reasons, its called living and loving, many things making up the whole.

March 28

The last 24 hours have been so good Keith, you would have loved it. Julian and Stefanie came on Saturday night and left tonight on their way to Dover and then the drive back home to Germany. In that time we have eaten, talked, laughed and yes we also cried. We missed you, I kept thinking how much you would have enjoyed being together.

You know what its like when Julian is around, slightly chaotic and lots of talking, about anything and everything. Adrian came and had lunch with us and that also filled out. Stefanie and I are getting to know each other much better, we've seen more of each other lately, and her conversation is also a good match for Julian.

Our discussion went from memories of you, Africa, Iraq, and because we went to the Persian restaurant again, Persia and its ancient history, church politics, homosexuality, cars, the future, gangsters, yes gangsters. Julian said there was one at the table near us.

I just felt so stimulated and grateful, grateful that in our three sons there is so much of you and that they are an amalgam of us, you and me, and part of us and them will always go on in the genetic pattern that has been made by our, yours and my amalgamation.

Yes, of course we also talked of philosophy because we're interested in it, apart that its Julian's especial interest.

You would like to see me animated, you'd probably say "old crinkle eyes". Yes, a good 24 hours and I hope and pray it will continue to encourage me to go forward.Love you lots and lots, night.

March 29

Just had a phone call from Julian, they are safe and sound back in Germany, having enjoyed themselves here. It was good, and has done me good. I feel exhilarated and energised – its because I used my brain.

What I plan and hope to do now is one thing, one outing, something that is different, takes me away from home, that stretches my mind. Don't know what, but I will look and try.

Today I was taken out for coffee to the garden centre and I enjoyed that because I have plans for the garden and you know how I enjoy that, totally different, it will no longer be a 'garden' because it isn't, it will be what it is. A terrace. This will be fun and a challenge especially as I have no money for it.

Anyway, I'm really tired, so I'm off to bed. It's this clock change, it always makes life hard to start with.

Night darling.

31st March

Just cleared the study. So much paper, but as today I have heartache, work is good. Once again I have a clear desk, letters answered etc., so while I wait for the vegetables to cook I'll write to you.

This Saturday is a year since we buried you. I wish these remembrances didn't come at weekends. So much easier to keep busy when everything is open and people are around. So I will probably, if its dry, go for a walk, read a lot, watch TV and eat chocolate and miss you, and miss you, and miss you. Oh, there goes the pinger for my vegetables, talk later.

April 2010

Good Friday, April 2

On the radio tonight was a programme called at the 'foot of the cross'. Readings and music. I listened because it's music you used to love, Karl Jenkins, Rutter etc. It was the most powerful programme. The readings were read with what I can only call restrained feeling, but passionate as well.

The picture that your mind drew was more telling than anything I've heard before. It was really telling the story of Christ and His death in a way that was more vivid than crosses, icons, any of these things that we grew up with.

To say I enjoyed it would be wrong, but that it touched me quite deeply would be correct.

To listen to that tonight with your music, the music that gave you so much pleasure, at Easter weekend and tomorrow being a year since we buried you, was very emotional.

I do hope and pray that I was always what you wanted and that I did for you all that you needed. It was always done with the utmost love.

Yes, at this time I am sad, very sad, not that the word SAD actually explains the pain and ache that I feel without you.

But thank God we both believe in a resurrection and we shall be together again, without your pain, all made new.

I love you darling and I do so miss you.

Saturday April 3 Easter weekend

Last night, I slept well, no dreams, just sleep, so this morning I am able to face the world.

April 2010

This time a year ago 'we laid you to rest', in your case that is what you needed and it has of course coloured my grief. Not the awful shock of sudden death, disease, or accident, just going to rest. Hence I think my grieving is perhaps a calmer experience.

Today is the last of my milestones, and looking back I can see that these milestones do help. They give a focus, a focus for remembering and enjoying 'being' with you, but also I imagine its also a time for letting go, which I'm not sure whether I do or don't. A bit like taking an exam to see whether one has learnt a bit more on your chosen subject.

Since last weekend with the family I am aware that I do have a future without you by my side. I can 'do' things, without transport it's more difficult but maybe the extra effort will be good for me. So long as my knee and foot don't pack up. One thing I am going to do is go to the theatre once a month. I hope.

This month the Welsh National Opera are here in Milton Keynes and I think I shall go and see Carmen. It's not an opera I particularly like, so to see it performed well will be good for me. You wouldn't like it though, would you?

Quite good though, our divergence on some music, but tolerance as well, just like life really.

I've just rung Julian to tell him the boat race is on today, unfortunately he can't pick it up anywhere, but I'll ring him with the result. Cambridge have lost the last 4-5, so maybe this year … . (They won by 1 ½ lengths!)

One year ago to the day darling we buried you. Today Adrian and I stood by your grave, not as cold as a year ago, but wet underfoot and the clay was sticky, but we have come through this year.

Never ever forgotten by us and others, but we are still here and must go on going on. I'm sure if I could speak to you, you would know what I am burbling on about.

I must not wallow, and also that is not in my nature, but I do feel that I must use today as a marker, for me to get on and do/be something. I must live before I die, and I hope that what is in front of me is something for the good of others, but also good for me.

After we came from your grave the family took me to the canal and the park that you and I had been to. We fed the ducks today as you and I did before. The weeping willow was beautiful and the daffodils were in full flower. It was lovely, and I thought I myself must 'go and do' different things otherwise I will be bored and boring, perish the thought!

Tomorrow, Easter Sunday, I've been offered a lift to church, which I look forward to and then we are going out to lunch, so I must build on this.

I love you, miss you, and want you, but I can't have you, so, I go it alone; but knowing always that this would be your wish for me.

The family have given me a lovely Easter egg and card, with lots and lots of love.

Even Bethany who is 4 on Monday said 'Papa was sick wasn't he? Papa has gone away.' It's so lovely that she remembers you, I'm so pleased.

Julian of Norwich said 'All will be well, all manner of things shall be well'. It's true darling all will be well, and so shall I. Good night, sleep well.

April 2010

4th April, 2010, Easter Sunday

A bad night again. In spite of trying a variation of pills and potions. It feels like someone is ploughing my brains up – really painful and debilitating. My eyeballs feel like organ stops being pushed and pulled.

However, another day. Yesterday was good. It was nice to have a meal at Ike and Sophia's and good conversation. So long as we are not 'criticizing' the church but trying to see and understand why it is not doing the job that God tells us to do. Ergo – visit the sick, in this instance, my husband. I do know that criticism has always been one of my faults. I pray that I maybe be aware of this and unless I can help the person or situation that I should keep my mouth closed.

It was good to see Ike and Sophia have a) worked at a good marriage, and what a fine son they have produced. B) The commitment to church and God, and their outreach programme to others.

In the midst of this, I pray that I may find a role for my remaining years.

My brain needs filling, using, after years of starving. With Keith's pain and inabilities many years have passed without any input except from ourselves. I know that we both looked for 'something' else. But all Keith got was more suffering – hard. I pray that I did what was right for him.

Now for today. Easter Sunday, the day of resurrection. This day is a day of real hope. My Keith only sleeps – please God that I might so live that we meet again and be together for ever. Our degrees of grief and sorrow vary, but the one thought of all of us has been, we lost YOU a long time ago. The dying was the end of a long beginning. The person we loved and love is a very dear memory, and always will be, but, in our minds you and me are at a certain stage of rest now.

April 7

I have gone through the Easter weekend and have enjoyed having my own company, and lots of good times and unusually something on the television to watch, art and music.

Then today, Wendy our artist teacher took us to the university library to look at their art department, and we were able to borrow books. I took one on Munch, Spencer and a book of African art, so I'm starting to grow darling.

Then Carrie and I are going to a concert one week and a ballet the next. Tomorrow, Gordon and Rosy are coming for a couple of hours to pick up some pots that I'm getting rid of.

Now I have decided that the space outside is a terrace not a garden, I need to alter most of the ideas and plants to make it like a terrace at a big house, or an Italian one.

Once again I'm writing in the middle of the night, it seems I sleep until about 1:30, then I'm awake until about 4, then I might get some sleep if I'm lucky. That's OK. if I don't have anything to do the next day. Unfortunately, tomorrow is busy right through. Some meetings and people coming here to see me.

April 2010

Saturday 10th April

I haven't written this week because for some reason I don't understand, I'm weeping, so sad is my head and my heart. It's as though you have just died, not a year ago. I just want to weep, to weep as opposed to cry. To 'weep' is so much deeper it seems to me than just to cry.

Nothing I can do this week can make this intense sadness and aloneness go away. I miss you darling.

Twice this week I've been told how very special you were. I loved and do still love you very much, but you and I seemed ordinary. We were blessed with a love for each other, but did I also see this 'specialness' or did I just see 'you', and I loved you?

It would be nice to talk this over with you. Certainly you never thought you were special, just you, and I loved just you.

Today I also found out that someone we both knew is not expected to live long, he is dying the same way as you, and my heart aches for him, his wife and family, and also for myself.

To me, it seems the feeling of being bereft gets worse, not better. Sometimes I really feel an ache in my head and heart, that are not just figures of speech. To help myself along, I keep busy, doing things, planning for the future, assuming this will help and I shall get better. I don't.

However, today has been a really warm spring day and as well as walking to the lake I've been gardening. Like most British people, one sunny day makes a summer, so I did some planting, tonight there will be a ground frost!

April 2010

What I've done though, you would have liked. As I said before, I now recognise that our little terrace, is just that, not a garden, so things have been disposed of and it actually looks good. To complete the picture I need a couple of bold statement plants or statues, something anyway to finish it off and then maybe, this year, I can sit in the sun and not work.

While I'm writing this I'm crying because I've lost what I really only ever wanted from life, you. Goodnight darling, I love you.

12th April
Been to the vampire today, well, to the surgery to get blood taken. Actually she's very good. Always manages to find a vein straight off, this time not even any bruising.

The weather has altered again, it's back to cold winds. I'm actually cold tonight, have just put a blanket on the bed. Sometimes I miss my feather duvet, but as it's only a single it's not much use.

Next day
Carrie and I 'did' the 3 garden centres today, needless to say I can hardly walk now. I imagine when I see the orthopaedic chap next week, he'll suggest surgery. Oh well I can't walk properly now so I suppose it will have to be done.

The 'terrace' is really taking shape now, I'm hoping that Gordon will be able to come and help me finish it and perhaps this year I can 'sit' in the garden and not work it all the time.

I'm very tired darling so I'm going to bed.
Goodnight darling.

16th April

Since I wrote last time the weather has reverted
to cold and very windy, a cold wind and because
it's a north wind it is also bringing the outpourings
of the volcano eruption from Iceland. Seeing the
progress on charts on the TV it's easy to see the
way the fallout would have been on the mountains
of Wales from the Chernobyl fallout.

These sort of happenings always to me
underline the fact that we human beings do not,
'rule the world', it rules us. It's very interesting to
see the interaction of so much of nature. We seem
to be having so many earthquakes around the
world, as if it is fed up with our mismanagement.

Today a friend's husband died as you did with
prostate cancer. It brings it all back to me and I
really do feel for her, because no one can really
help in these circumstances, however close the
family, we all have to walk this part alone.

When I go past your photograph I still find it
difficult to understand that you are really gone; not
here. That I will never see you again, and I can
only look at you and say 'I love you'.

But we were blessed, we had most of our life
together, and for that I was grateful. I do still love
you the person who was always my other half. Bit
like the phantom pain of an amputee, the limb isn't
there but oh does it hurt.

But I am stronger and more of life is being
lived. Tomorrow I'm going to the theatre to see an

Alan Bennett play, and I'm hoping to be able to go out more soon.

I do read a lot, just finished a book by John McCarthy and Brian Keenan. 10 years after their release from captivity in Iraq they did a trip which they had planned while in captivity, it was informative, funny, and sad, a book that actually makes you as a person grow a little.

When you were ill I read detective stories, it was necessary for me to escape into a different world. It rested both my brain and my body. Now, I can't read fiction, it has to be reality.

I find life, and now of course death, very interesting, to see and be aware of changes and the reason for these changes, mostly in one's self, is like reading a story, you begin, go on with the story, and suddenly you reach the end. Close the book and start another. 'C'est la vie'.

However, each story of mine I perceive ends with the same words, I love you. Goodnight darling.

21st April

Honestly darling, how can I lose so many things in a 5-roomed flat? [Liz has included the bathroom and kitchen in the count.] This is something I seem to do a lot. Today it's my bra! Usually I have to turn everything out, today is no different. In fact I had lost this diary that I'm writing in. Obviously I found it, under something else. Whether all this is years of stress and strain or the effects of grieving, I don't know, but it is exhausting.

April 2010

I am, at the moment, sitting on our terrace (with bra on), it's a lovely day and the plants look really good now, you would like it, although I think the breeze would be a bit chilly for you.

Alex has gone to have lunch with friends so I'm going up to see that Michael is all right while she's out, therefore my writing will be quite fragmented.

23 April, St George's Day

I learnt yesterday that today is the last day to pick dandelions for dandelion wine. After this it is very difficult to get the pollen out of the wine, lots of sieving, etc. My mum used to make wines, as a child I used to hear tops exploding if the wine wasn't bottled properly.

Do wish that we took more notice of things that happened in our childhood, so much has been lost. The other day Carrie and I saw big round pots and I said I remembered my mother preserving eggs in those big pots with Essen glass. Carrie had never known anyone else who knew about this, and she is 14 years younger than me.

It's Friday today, well, at the moment it's Friday morning 5:10 am. I've been awake for 2 hours and can't go back to sleep. At 8 o'clock my new chair is arriving. I think you would have a fit if you were here. Never have I spent so much on anything, but this does have a massager in the body of the chair, and a heater!

It is, of course, a recliner, so I can get some proper rest. Do hope it's okay. It's like the one you had, goes up and down, but it has extras and also made for my size -- small, in other words. So I will be able to sit comfortably and relax and watch all the 'hoo ha' about the election!

I know you would have enjoyed it all, the election, and snooker is on as well. I think of you so many times, its 'Keith would like that' or 'Keith did that' and so on and so on. But all my thoughts are pleasant, memories of a life well-lived.

I'm going back to bed for an hour as they are delivering the chair at 8:00, hope I wake up in time. Love you lots.

Later. Yes, the chair came, and it was wrong, it would have fitted you, so consequently, for me it's too big. Oh dear.

Saturday 24th April

Whenever I think I am 'all right' suddenly quite unconsciously a deep, deep sadness hits me and I want you. I think I can manage, and it's OK. being on my own – but it isn't and I miss you, dreadfully.

Today is such a day. I just want to cry because I'm sad and alone. I do so miss you. I would like to be with you. Nothing on this earth calls me as much as you do darling.

I'm sure I didn't know how much I loved you till you died. After 59 years we just were, we knew we loved each other and needed each other, but for me at least, I don't think I knew how much.

Do you remember the Kathleen Ferrier song 'What is Life to Me Without Thee?' Well, I think that song was written by someone in this situation, especially after all these years.

April 2010

Wednesday 28th April

It seems ages since I wrote to you but its only 4 days ago, life does seem hectic sometimes, and this week has been busy.

Things to go to, things to do, none of them exciting, but time consuming. One day I helped in the village to sort clothes for the spring fair. That was a busy day. Then shopping for food, waiting for my chair to be delivered, only to find its wrong, so another wait for them to remove it.

Today has been good, Gordon came while Rosemary was at a meeting and did a lot in the garden for me, and now it really is almost ready to sit in (I hope) just as you would say, my finishing touches!

Also it was nice because the two boys were here together and we went out for lunch, so good conversation.

What does surprise me though is how weepy I am lately, only little weeps, but they come quite out of the blue. The loss of you goes very, very deep and I suppose always will until we're together again. I love you darling, that is all I can say, but oh, it means so much.

Today we planted up your Johnson Blue geranium and some achemechia molls, places round the terrace where I can 'see' you.

At the garden centre the other day with Carrie I saw Gunnera, but even I can't find a place for a Gunnera on a stone terrace with no soil and burning sun, perhaps I should try cacti!

Did I say I've started a fitness programme at the gym? I think I do feel better for it, somehow more alert and my knees are less painful as well.

Hopefully as I'm also eating properly I will lose some weight. I'll never be 17 again but a least I hope I won't have quite so many 'wobbly bits.'

This week is Africa week on TV so I'm off to watch one of 4 programmes on tonight, this is about the Soweto String Quartet, as we have 3 of their CD's it should be interesting to watch.

Night darling.

May 2010

May 1st

Hello darling.

Well for me this has been the weekend of the spring fair. Carrie has taken me out to art galleries and Leigh has taken me out to choose a chair.

It started with 2 days of 'sorting' through all the donations, bric-a-brac, clothes, tombola, shoes, books, it took over 2 days just to get some order into the whole proceedings and the pricing up, but I did enjoy it. As you know I don't like doing 'front of house', but I'm a good sorter.

Yesterday was the actual fair, and it went very well and plenty of money was raised for various good causes.

Leigh took me out to find a comfortable chair, and we did just one shop and found exactly my size chair, my feet actually touch the floor, and I fell in love with the matching sofa, just the right size and length for me to have a doze on.

I really think you would approve and I wish we had had something more comfortable for you to rest your poor body in. I'm so sorry we didn't, but we weren't to know how painful your body would get. I'm so sorry darling.

However, I do think you would like my choice now. Then today Carrie took me to see what she thought, and she liked it and she understands the room proportions. For someone who said she would never have leather, this is in fact leather, and, well, I reckon at 77 and getting older, it would be easier to wipe down if I have an accident.

After that we went to Beaconsfield to the art gallery that she is part of, I don't think there was anything you would have liked, a sculpture caught my eyes but it was £300 so it stayed there. Two gannets doing their courting dance, lovely and well worth the money.

On our way home we stopped at a children's farm and fed the goats and small animals, and in this complex was a really good art and gift shop. They had some really beautiful objects well made, very different and very cheering. I brought a lovely plate with cave paintings for Liz's birthday and a heron for me – well, for the garden. It's really very lovely, and again, you would love it, but most of all it's made in Africa, Zimbabwe, made from old petrol drums, beaten and given a bronze patina. Remember all the packing we did in those drums first time to Africa? [In 1967 when we first went to Nigeria, by sea, we packed goods and chattels into 40-gallon oil barrels with salt water-proof seals and locks on the lids.]

I'm going to make a pseudo pond and stand the heron by it, and it will make the terrace. The final piece of design I think.

I so wish you were here to see and enjoy what I'm doing. You've always had pleasure from your home and garden. This week I've also helped, I hope, 2 women whose husbands have just died, you see darling, even in death you are helping others.

Only because of my own journey through pain can I understand and help others. You were a good man, and made me able to impart help to others. I'm tired love, goodnight.

May 2010

3rd May Bank Holiday Monday

Last night I dreamt of you. We were together choosing things for the house, it was lovely to have the dream of us as we were. Probably because yesterday I was choosing things for our house I suppose.

I have a photo of you on my desk and it's so you, smiling with your eyes, smiling mouth as well. When you think of the heartache all over the world of women looking at a picture of a dead (I hate that word) husband, it's a wonder that the world doesn't just crack open with the pain of loss. I say women because this is the pain I know, but of course there is so much more.

I don't think I could bear it if death was the end. No hope, awful thought, and we in this country have so much to be thankful for. Yes, our forces are in dangerous situations and any death decreases me, but those chaps did choose their life and knew that death could come.

Illness and disease we have no choice, but I am so glad I could nurse you at home. Please God it made it just that little easier for you. But dead or not darling, I love you still very much.

Just now on the radio they've played 'The trout' one of our favourites.

We are in May but judging by the weather its March or April, north wind, showers, sunshine, just needs hail and snow and we would have gone through the year's weather.

Adrian and his family will be over today to visit, but while they're here they change the bed for me, I can't lift the mattress to tuck sheets in.

I do hate being a weak and feeble woman! My heart isn't but my body is.

8th May

Just woken up after a reasonable night but can't relax, so here I am.

It has been for me an emotional time. Adrian and Sue's car needs a lot of work done on it and there is no money, and you know how that preys on me.

Anyway, Julian came up with a good idea, we just get it through the MOT and they will run it until it stops dead, maybe a month, maybe a year, so that's what it looks like. I wish you were here to help my mind, 'it'll be all right' you'd say, and it usually was, but you aren't here and it isn't.

Our weather is still awful, a cold, cold wind and not much sunshine. This last week you would have enjoyed, the General Election, which has been going on forever, and just ended as we all thought, a hung parliament. So what the way forward is, no one seems to know.

All 3 parties don't want to work with each other and Brown won't step down. Whether all the small parties will support Brown, at a cost for their own areas, who knows.

I did vote, but without a lot of hope of any of them. You would like it wouldn't you if we got proportional representation. Don't know what I would like, but not American style government, we are British.

Carrie was going to take me to the grave today but it's very wet underfoot, so that clay would be awful. I need to measure for your 'name plate' which Gwyn is getting done in Wales for me. The clay just makes our shoes so heavy, so it will probably be tomorrow.

I am going to have what I hope will be a quiet day, my head aches very badly. Mostly this week I think it's unshed tears, not for me although that comes into it, but for, and because of others.

I think I'm going to just throw clothes on and get my paper and then crawl into bed, maybe stay there and rest my mind and body.

May 10th

Oh, I could do with a cuddle, so many things pressing in on me at the moment. I wish you were here to love me and steer me through these woods. I consider myself not a blubber, but I do – pause here for a quick sniff and nose-blowing. Wonder if there is an article somewhere on pain, in all its guises? A broken leg would hurt like mad, but one can take pills for that and you know it will go away. Heart pain is not hurting pain but for me, and ever present ache? Weight? hollowness? Don't know why it hurts and hurts.

I was going to change tune and tell you how the weather has been, but I would be lying, it's very cold. North winds etc., by now we should all be sitting out and getting brown, no such luck, indoors and heat on.

One thing you would love is that 'our hosta' is out, beautiful big leaves, it so reminds me of your and our pleasure making a garden at Cae Du. Our trees on the terrace are all in full leaf and beautifully fresh looking. When I sit by the window and see our terrace full of green, I'm happy, it is the way we planned it together.

Tonight I have a sore throat, headache and cough, so I will say goodnight and take myself 'awa to my bed'. See you in the morning, love you.

Next day

It's just a day later, May 11th I think, and it is cold. I still put the heating on and quite high at that, we are all heat and sun starved. Apparently Moscow is -30, I don't think I like this global warming if that's what it is, even the trees look cold.

One thing you would love is the cowslip are everywhere in great profusion this year, everyone is amazed at the number.

Today I went to the grave, Carrie took me, and the dog was with us, so she took him for a walk in the little Park next to the graveyard, the grass was just full of cowslips, don't think I've seen this since I was a child. Beautiful, and all next door to you!

The whole reason for going to the grave was to put some fertilizer on the edging to encourage the lichen to grow on the edging, and to get your pot and replant it. This time I'm going to put (?) in and it won't hurt if we don't get rain. We're having it all now, and for the next few nights, frosts, and it's May.

Gordon Brown stood down today from Prime Minister and we are in the midst of a sort of hung parliament. You would have enjoyed all the election 'hoo hah' and it's going to go on now, even longer. Do wish the media would not always look to pull people down.

I do think even though I'm not Labour that he has tried his best. I certainly think that what you see is what you get with him. So now we have to go through all this again, but yes you would have enjoyed this election and its follow-on.

My ulcer hurts today so I'm going to bed now, with hot milk and a book. Night darling.

Tuesday 11th May

Usually I write to you at night before I go to bed, today it is only 6pm, light, it is a spring evening, well it would be if we didn't have such low temperatures. I'm really cold.

Missing you seems to take all forms, today I wanted to cry because I couldn't wrap this present for Liz properly. You would always make sure that whatever it was arrived in one piece. To pack this dish I've bought, Liz needs two boxes cut down and padded and sealed, and I just can't do it, and I'm afraid I cried, for you, for so many reasons, I miss you and love you.

If the weather is good tomorrow??? I should plant up the pot from the grave so it withstands rain and sun.

It must seem as though my life is all to do with missing you, yes of course, that is a large part of it after nearly 60 years together, but I think to other people I'm 'all right', it's the very private part of me that hurts, and that's why I write. I know you understand, just as you have over all these years.

May 2010

12th May (My mother's wedding anniversary)

Well darling, I'm not sure what my future holds, I'm reduced to knitting a scarf for a teddy bear! My own choice. The teddy I won at the fair had a bright red floppy bow, awful thing so I took it off and decided I would knit one.

Now I've decided to do it in Oxford and Cambridge colours. As I say, I really must find a future somehow. This is probably the slippery slope to senility. However, I am keeping up my gym work. 3 times a week, about half an hour, can't see any weight off, but I think that's because my thyroid is up the creek. Tomorrow I see my doctor and hope something can be sorted out.

This morning I went shopping with Margaret, who is completely blind. She actually took me shopping, knew where things were in M & S and got the taxi organised. Did better than I did, she is 10-12 years younger, but even so, she's brilliant.

When I sit here at my desk writing I keep looking up to your photo, you were a happy soul, even in pain you didn't moan, a good man and I wish you were here for me to tell you so. Love you.

Another thing you'd be surprised at is, I've been watching the news, mainly because of Gordon Brown's 'stand down' and because in actual fact I know little about politics. So I've watched his resignation and the signing up of 'the pact.' Overall I rather like the idea that we have young men at the helm. Very well educated men and a change now to me seems a good way forward. If you were here we could really have some good discussions. You would have so enjoyed the inner workings, having been at the helm yourself so often.

As I get older, I really seem to be widening my life. Partly of course, this is because I actually have time now. All I have to think about is me. One of the plus outcomes of this situation is now that my skin is so good I have time to take care of myself. Suppose it's the old adage, 'it's an ill wind that blows …' etc., etc.

15th May

Last night I couldn't get to sleep so did some jobs, tidying up, etc. One of the bookshelves had photo albums and I went through them, looking at pictures of you. I realised how good looking and happy you were, and I saw the lovely smile that people always comment on.

Sometimes we don't see what is in front of us.

I loved you. I've always liked you, the way you looked and dressed, etc., but only now can I see deeper into you, and that's what I miss so much. The deep person inside, and of course at the end and for many years before the end, you had started to leave, I was your nurse, checking, altering, always looking for a way that would be better.

Reminds me of that poem 'The Road Less Taken'. [Liz seems to mean 'The Road Not Taken' by Robert Frost] We had no choice, the road was the only one we had to travel, looking back it was very long, and I think for both of us, lonely – we were different, but still us.

What I think I am saddest about is losing you, in every sense, and just lately that sadness and loneliness is very hard. I keep having what I call 'little weeps' – just deep sadness.

I so miss you and love you, but I'm glad we did have love.

May 15th (continued)

Also yesterday Adrian and Sue took me to the bluebell woods. Last time we went there with you in the wheelchair, you also got out and walked a bit. You poor thing, I don't think any of us really knew how much you suffered. I'm sorry.

The bluebells were wonderful, so many, spreading under the trees, into the distance and such a deep blue this year. I walked down the path where we had been and just had a quiet weep, not crying, just tears rolling down my cheeks. I am so lonely at times and long for your love.

All sorts of things have been happening just lately that I have to take decisions on. I keep saying to myself, 'what would Keith say? what would Keith do?' Always I 'hear' you saying 'don't worry, it will be alright' or 'just leave it, it will sort itself out'.

So many things happen that make me relate to you. I read today about a person who always answered a question in the Talmudic way, with another question. Remember how cross I used to get at that. You were much more Jewish than you knew. I suppose not knowing until you're 50 or so, there must have been lots of things you yourself didn't understand.

You always wanted to go to one of the concentration camps, you said, just to acknowledge what others had suffered. Something inside you must have produced these thoughts, feelings, etc.

Poor darling, both of us had unacknowledged hurts. Me trying to forget my childhood, and only living when I met you. And you having no idea that you were indeed a different person from the inside out. What a couple! Thank God you are at peace now. I just wish my heart had some peace. Love you lots darling.

So something in both of us reacted to the unknown need of the other. When I said I didn't want to remember my childhood and all these years you never asked me to talk about it. You were a good man. You always said you got better than you knew, with me. It's only now you are dead that I can see and must say, I had better than I knew.

Can't remember who wrote it, but "Love does not alter when it alteration finds. It is an ever fixed mark". Your death if anything just underlines how much love we had, that even now without putting you on a pedestal, it's a love that is very deep and real. It is an ever fixed mark.

Must go and look up who wrote that. … Got it, Shakespeare, sonnet 116:

Let me not to the marriage of true minds
Admit impediments. Love is not love
Which alters when it alteration finds,
Or bends with the remover to remove.
O, no, it is an ever fixed mark,
That looks on tempests and is never shaken … .

I did think it might have been Herrick, but I was wrong, about the poet, not the feeling.

May 2010

I am going to bed now, goodnight darling.

19th May

At last, sunshine, really hot and bright, a day for doing nothing but sitting still. When we do get to summer, I really think we'll be too hot.

Yesterday I took the newly planted pot to your grave. Maybe it seems silly to give you plants, but if you were alive, you'd like it, so I do it.

I really am managing very well, people say that I'm amazing, actually I think we all at different times, lie, just by being – heartache and loneliness don't show. No that's not true, they do, but only certain people can actually see pain, and today I had two people give me a hug. They 'saw' I needed it. But interestingly, as I thanked one of them for the hug, they said, 'it's not just for you, I need a hug too'.

How little we know about each other sometimes. I must try to be more aware of others.

Friends, B & C were up from Bala today, and it was lovely to see them. We had lunch here today and tomorrow we are having a meal out and then to the theatre, so a busy day.

I am always saying to you how much I love you, and I do. Goodnight darling.

23rd May

Yesterday Rosemary was ordained to the ministry. I saw it on the computer, 3 women were ordained to full Pastors, you would have enjoyed watching it. Peter Lockey is at SEC [South England Conference of the Seventh Day Adventist Church; we three boys were at school with Lockey.]

and he mentioned that Gordon and Rosy's fathers were both Pastors.

That made me weep a little bit. I do so wish you were here. So much to show you and tell you.

[No date, between the 23rd and 29th May]

Haven't written for some time because it has been a horrible few days. I've missed you and your wisdom. And now the fridge has packed up. I wander around thinking 'what would Keith do?' and although it's a long time since you did the coping, at least we could talk it through and then I'd deal with it. Now I have to try and work out the pros and cons myself.

Last night I woke at 3:30 and as usual staggered into the kitchen for a drink, only to find the fridge was not cold! The heat has been intense these last few days, especially in the kitchen. I think it just can't cope. Whether the freezer has given up as well, I don't know as they run as two separate entities.

Finding someone to repair it is very hard. By the time you've paid out a call out fee and the work it probably will be the same as a new fridge. So this afternoon, I just put my head on the desk and cried, then got up and coped as usual.

A quick cry does help though. I've still got to work out the problems but I'm not so fraught. Part of the problem today is that the humidity is high and that for me always was difficult.

I'm now going to watch Chelsea Flower Show, and 'damn everybody'. [For Liz, this is a Churchill quote: So the story goes, when things got too much, at bed time he would put his head under the blankets, utter this phrase with emphasis and feel the better for it.]

29th May

Such a long time since I wrote, sorry, but so many things going wrong I don't know where to start. Re the fridge, I was so blessed to find a refrigeration engineer, which I didn't know I needed. He came, took it to pieces, and explained what was wrong, a manufacturing fault! A piece missing! What on earth are we buying sight unseen?

He suggested I ring the manufacturer and complain, which I will probably do now I'm less fraught. Anyway I now have a fridge and freezer working, no need for a new one. But think, that might have meant spending £400. These are the things I panic about, things I don't understand.

On top of that I seem to have been in pain from head to foot for the last couple of weeks. But today I have done something unusual, I stayed in bed, giving my whole body a rest, and apart from the fact I have no chocolate(!), I am much better. I read, slept, read, ate, slept, and now I'm trying to clear up a bit at the desk, and unusually for us lately, it's raining. The garden will be happy, so am I, carrying watering cans hurts.

This coming week I'm going to London to see the Ife exhibition with Gordon, My mother's day present. I'll tell you later.

The other thing I'm doing, as well is I've borrowed a projector and I'm going to look at some of our African slides. Maybe looking at so many memories will help me to remember some of the many good times we had together. I'm really looking forward to that and the Ife heads. Lots of memories, lots of living, lots of love.

This week I'm also writing to Currie Wanderer, via Bob Southey, to ask if she remembers staying with us and cooking pancakes with Amy? [These were students from America who came over to do church work for a year.] We really used to enjoy the youngsters didn't we. I do miss that. I need to mix more with younger people.

I do miss you darling, and as I look at the slides, I still have two things near me, Tissues and chocolates. Love you.

Later: Just off to bed after a really restful day, looked at your photo by the bed and said goodnight. It was taken 5-6 years ago, still my handsome husband, only I knew you were not you, but you have your lovely smile in the picture, and I am getting older and more lonely. Not that the word lonely is correct, much more that I am alone, without you. We had a good life darling, we were lucky.

30th May

Another week with three Sundays, I really do not like Bank Holidays, too much time and nothing to do.

This week is Ife week and up to the British Museum. Wonder if we will see any Nigerians there? Maybe in their robes, that would be nice.

I feel better about going now because Adrian is coming with me. I'm not brave enough to 'do' London on my own. Not that I will do it often enough to get used to it. Now I'm really looking forward to it.

May 2010

Tomorrow is the first of June, and I've got the heating on! Will we have any summer?

3rd June

An absolutely superb day. The boys took me to the British Museum to see the exhibition on the 'Ife' Head. It brought back so many memories of our life in West Africa, the sense of worth of the job we were doing. The boys growing up in natural surroundings and just the joy of being together and doing a good job. I've always said that Africa used every part of our being, body, mind, and spirit. Good days.

Particularly I wished you had been with us as we went through the Egyptian rooms, and the Mesopotamian area. It really fed some of my mental needs for stimulation, you would have loved it.

Adrian came with me on the train, we got a taxi to the British Museum, Gordon met us there. He took me around the exhibition in a wheelchair and Adrian went to the Islamic rooms that really interested him. I was looked after, it was no strain either physical or mental, a really, really lovely day.

I know that you would be pleased to see me happy and stimulated. Once when you were ill we had a visitor, you said to me, 'it was lovely to see you animated again.' I was on this day darling, but oh, it would have been wonderful to have shared it with you.

It seems most peculiar to say that I love you more now, but it is so, maybe after 10 years of nursing you, I really did in every sense lose you over that period. Now looking back, I can see and remember the you that was you. Whatever – I do love you.

Do you think it's silly writing you letters? I feel that you would like them and one day you'll answer them. Your letter writing was lovely, always made me feel very special. Like a lot of men, you could write better than you spoke.

I've been a very blessed girl/woman. Thanks for all that, love you.

[No Date]
After a week of kerfuffling, Adrian and Sue have their 'new' old car.

It is old but it's in very good condition and more comfortable than the other one. This one is a ¼ of what it would have cost to fix the other one, and at the price they paid, there's enough in the bank for a buffer if anything goes wrong. Maybe now we can have a break from 'worry.'

I saw the consultant for my eyes today, in two weeks I have my right eye done, 6 weeks later the other one. Although I'm scared it will be good to read properly again. Now I'm able to understand what you went through.

Soon it is Father's Day, and I have bought you a present, a sketch of a gymnast having a rest, a pencil sketch. I shall hang it in the sitting room under the one you call 'Dear John.' You would like it I'm sure, and it's still part of a collection of nudes/backs.

Next week is our mini budget, we all wait to see exactly what the cuts are and who will hurt the most. One would think that the old age pension would be safe, hope it is, I do manage, but nothing left for real luxury.

Eyes are closing now, will go and see if I can sleep, love you.

11th June

Haven't written for a few days because I've had such a heartache. I dreamt that you and I were in bed, cuddling and talking as we used to enjoy doing, and the reality when I woke and you weren't there – you were dead! Awful wakening.

Sounds dramatic but I felt as though a piece of my heart had been ripped out, it took me days to find some relief from the pain.

Dreams can be so real can't they, and then to wake up and lose you again. Horrible.

Then tonight I watched 'La Bohème' and I cried. I didn't think it would touch me, but others' sorrow and sadness starts me off. The production was very good, it was a film as opposed to a stage production so the 'sets' were much more varied. Don't suppose you would have enjoyed it, maybe the music but not watching.

I love you darling and I do so want you but I know we shall be together again one day, but getting through the here and now is very hard. Some days are good and I'm okay, but some days the ache is bad. As it is for everyone, I know that, but … my pain is my pain.

Today I started on the cross trainer at the gym. I go three times a week now, trying to lose weight. Weight doesn't seem to be moving but I feel as though I am getting toned up. And I'm trying not to eat chocolate, it's very hard.

It is now June and so far this month I've put the heating on twice!

18th June

While it is some time since I last wrote, you have been in my thoughts so much.

This week I go to have a cataract done, just in time as I am having difficulty seeing, but of course, you had a worse problem than me, but now I understand you more, and I'm sorry for you.

If – and it certainly isn't what I want for you, but – I would have been different, hindsight, etc., I think I would not have fought for you so much, because I now realise you wanted to go much earlier. But we only got the one chance.

I love you darling and pray that I didn't in any way make you sad or hurt. Knowing you, you'd probably say 'don't worry about it', but I need absolution. As you can hear, I'm sad, very sad. Partly, I'm just very tired and in pain, and I'm frightened about my eyes, and there's no one to cuddle me, so I'm sorry for myself.

Your photograph is in front of me, the one when you were still able to smile. I wish I had that smile right now. I love you and miss the YOU, you were.

Last weekend I spent time going through your slides, that was quite fun, particularly the old ones when the boys were small. I've kept a few to look at again, and maybe have prints taken off them.

Because I won't be able to bend or lift after my eye is done, I've been working hard to get our garden 'done' then all I have to ask for help for is watering. The whole garden looks good, not a flower in sight, just green, but all a different green, very peaceful. You would love it I know.

June 2010

Even your grave is looking better, more settled and tended. In a couple of weeks, the plaque will be done as well. Fortunately, Sue saw that I'd made a mistake on the dates! Figures, me, numbers, maths!

There's very little TV worth watching because of the World Cup, so I'll have to really check the radio in the TV times, because I shan't be able to read. That is awful.

Just read an article about how losing one's sense of smell can be an early indication of Parkinson's. All knowledge is too late for you, but someone somewhere will benefit in the future. Your sense of smell went years before the diagnosis.

20th June

Adrian and family came over today for lunch, and we had butterbeans, which everyone enjoyed. [Anciently, a favourite family meal going back at least to Keith's grandma.]

Probably the first time since you died that we've had these, they were actually very nice, mushy and soft, just how your mother made them.

After that we went for a walk to the peace pagoda, and it was solstice day and they had a special service on, it was colourful and pleasant, just their deep drums, not just bang, bang, and cymbals and a gong, it was a pleasant day, nice to be together.

June 2010

June 26th

Well, I really don't know what the writing will be like, I've had my eye done and one eye is better, and one eye is bad, but my glasses are prismed for two bad eyes. You had the same problem when you had your eyes done. Unlike yours though, this really hurt, everyone I spoke to said 'it doesn't hurt'. It did. Very much.

I also expected that I would be able to get on with things, also no. I really feel as though I've been 'knocked about a bit'. Today is the third day and only now can I do something without falling asleep, and I today don't look white, just getting my old colour back.

So much reminds me of you. Everything looks so bright and clear with my new eyes. I was going to get the girl who cleans for me to wash all the doors down, they looked really grubby. Now of course, they look absolutely white, its good.

Wish I had you here to hold my hand. I need cosseting and there's no one to do that, I could do with putting my head on your big shoulders and being loved. Death does not just take your body away but also my emotional support in times of need.

Really I think I manage well, but oh, the ache of not having you. I'm still writing otherwise I'll bawl again.

Carrie and Alex have been good to me, shopping and dropping in, etc., lifting heavy things. Adrian and Sue are coming over to water the garden. All is not lost, I'm just like Lord Nelson; one eye.

June 2010

Next Day

Eye much better but balance not good. I do feel so much for you now, with all the problems you had, sorry darling. Not until you walk in someone else's shoes do we know how they hurt.

Sitting in the study with the window open and the evening of a beautiful day.

If you were here we would be going for a walk in the cool of the evening. As I sat in the garden and admired it and enjoyed the smell, I thought of you worrying how I would manage without you and that you were happy to leave me because I would be safe here and Adrian and Sue would look after me here at the village.

All that is right. As I sat in the garden, I counted my blessings. I am safe, enough money to manage, and a lovely little garden. This year I have no flowers in the garden, just greenery, and it is lovely, cool and calm. I am so grateful for everything, you have no need to worry, until I see you again all is well. My later years are good, and I am still in love with you, though my bed is without you. Rest my love, and I will too. Goodnight.

30th June

Because of this eye, can't put my head down, i.e. bending, I'm really stretched to 'do' anything. But today, I sorted a drawer. I found photos of our golden wedding. You were still 'my Keith' then although we knew you were ill and that it would get worse. I'm glad we took the day to celebrate. But what really made me cry and ache for life again, I found an autograph book you gave me when I was 17-18. I should have realized then, that you, not me were the writer, poet to the family. You expressed your love so well and so deeply, as young as we both were.

It's a shame we can't go round again with the knowledge that comes later. Thank you for my book and the love that is within it.

Do tears count as getting water in your eye? I mustn't cry in case I damage the work they've done. But oh, I want to. I love you.

Also today I saw Ike, I've also asked him to bury me, I'd like to be next to you. What the future holds I don't know, but today with all the best intentions in the world, it's a 'chocolate day' and now I feel sick; oh dear, I suppose it's better than alcohol!

Love you, sleep well.

July 2010

Sunday 4th July, Independence Day

Tonight I went to a concert with Carrie. If I had thought about it, I shouldn't have gone, music you loved was played, tears rolled, just tears, no one knew, and now I've just realized that I'm going to another one on Thursday – our anniversary. I don't think I can manage it and it wouldn't be fair to Carrie.

Your death, your not being here, is still so raw and real. I don't dwell on things but they come and hurt me just the same. I would love to have you here, for my own selfish sake. I want to be loved, to be held, and kissed and to lay in your arms and talk, we used to enjoy just lying and talking didn't we? Just close, is it really better 'to have loved and lost than never to have loved at all?' Can you feel pain for something you don't know the worth of? I only know I hurt, and miss you.

In two weeks Gwyn will come with your headstone, maybe after placing that I will find some peace, Oh, if only I could really say to you 'I love you' and hold you.

Sorry, I can't stop crying.

Sounds dramatic but I wish I was with you. I know neither of us would know, but I miss you, and I don't want to be big and strong, I'm not. I'm empty of all feeling but sadness.

5.7.10

Yesterday I heard of a book written by a woman whose husband had died, and she wrote him letters, just as I do to you. So I went and brought the book. We are different, she's young with young children, married 10 years. I'm old, grown up children and married 60 years. But grief is grief, from Adam and Eve onward, people have grieved, but it's still so new and raw when it happens to you.

Adrian and the family came today, I just couldn't bear to be with me. That might sound silly, but that's how I felt. Sue, Sara and Bethany went off to the park and Adrian and I went off and had a coffee and discussed money. He suggested that I made another account and had that just for paying the bills, DD's for instance.

It was a good idea and the girl at the bank sorted it all out, so now I can see what I'm doing, I think you would be proud of me. I certainly feel more comfortable, financially, because I can see what's going on. Also now online banking

The day has passed and I am at peace now, so long as I can now sleep. My eye hurts today, for the first time since the operation. I think I've read too much. Not to be able to read is awful, there's so many things I want to read.

6th July

Yes, I did sleep last night and only woke once. 6:30, got up, made tea, and then read.

The weather has been wonderful for 2-3 weeks now. I can't sit out though, the strong light hurts my eye, so I feel that I'm wasting it.

Carrie is taking me to your grave today, I feel I need to be near you. How can I say near you when we are worlds and worlds apart. But the little bit physically that is left of you, IS THERE. The rest of you is all around me, I do love you.

Back from going, that's Irish, but I've just woken from a 2-hour afternoon sleep!

First we went to Hobbycraft to get my acrylic paints and all the bits and bobs to go with it. Do hope this desire, or feeling rather, that maybe I can 'do' with this type of paint, works.

Then we went to your grave, it's looking tidier and we put in some saxifraga for you, tidied round the edges and I talked to you. I haven't been able to do that before. There's always someone with me. Carrie is sensitive enough to know what I need.

It doesn't seem strange at all writing to you, but to talk out loud at your grave did. Why?

After that we went back to Carrie's to pick up paint brushes for me. I still have all yours, but they are either watercolour or Chinese brushes. So sometime next week I'm going to Carrie's to start. She is very good to me.

I also like going because I get to pet Pongo the poodle. If there was some way to exercise the dog, I would have one again, well, maybe. Not with the cost of vet's bills now.

I have needed three things, 1. a good walk which we did through meadows to get to your grave, 2. to be 'near' you, 3. A good sleep, and it was, over 2 hours of deep dreamless sleep. Today the pain and longing for you is assuaged, for a while.

9th July
The day after our wedding anniversary. All the boys either rang or came to see me yesterday. Caring, as you would have wished for me, and in

the evening Adrian Sue and I went out for a meal, from me, to say thanks for all they do.

It actually was a good day. I am starting to live my life, not forgetting you, but being able to enjoy happenings without the 'guilt', I suppose, of you not being able to experience things as well.

At the concert last week, I kept thinking 'Keith would have liked this' and then another thought pushed into my head, 'what would you enjoy'? meaning me. It seems to me this might be the start of recovery, what do you think?

Tomorrow, Saturday, I go to another concert, all six of the Bach Brandenburg Concerto's. We go to Buckingham main church for this, and it is the Stowe Orchestra. This is a concert both of us would enjoy, and the following week a Flamenco evening, so I do get a life by virtue of good friends.

The intense heat we are experiencing is hard to cope with, I've got fans going everywhere all the time. Wish I had air conditioning tonight darling. I'm too tired to write, but I need this contact with you. Goodnight love.

Sunday 11th July

Having just come back from the 'outing' to the Milton Keynes Museum, and as it was advertised The Country Fair. Well, 6-7 stalls do not a country fair make. You might remember you and I went to the museum before we came here to Lovat Fields. You found it hard then, not able to walk properly. Today I remembered what we saw, but without too much pain.

Really I'd gone to give Alex some company and to see the fair, needless to say I was very disappointed, but it was, weather-wise, a nice day, and the temperature was down and a good breeze going.

One of the exhibits had a WWII garden, very 'dig for victory', 'grow your own food' etc., and an air raid shelter, like the one you dug out at one of our houses. Quite fun.

Last night the concert was superb, you would have so enjoyed it. I tried to do what you could do so easily. Identify the instruments, it was quite difficult because I couldn't see the whole orchestra. I must not sit behind tall people!

The solo parts by recorder were exquisite and it's the first time I've heard the harpsichord used as a solo instrument. Wonderful. I shall now go and find our recordings and play them. – I did and they were awful.

A very bad night so a cup of tea at about 4:00am, then out, so now, 3pm, I'm off to make a much needed cuppa. Love you lots and miss you lots, but, I think I'm growing up. I think you'd probably be proud of me. Luv 'n' stuff.

Monday 12th July

Every time I write the date I'm just amazed at the passing of time, over half the year gone, life does fly by.

Would you believe that today I don't know what to do with myself? I have a day in which I don't have to visit someone, talk to someone, be visited by someone, and I'm lost! There is nothing for me to do, and I just can't remember this happening to me for a very, very long time. I am lost. What makes it worse is with this cataract operation I can't do much and reading is quite difficult, dare I say I am bored?

What yesterday and today have done though is given me time to think about ME and my future. I am, and always will be, a 'doer' not a sitter, so, next step for Liz? Dunno.

Well I'm more serious about my writing so I think that for me the way forward is 'WORDS'. Encouragement has always come from you and the boys, but I'm not very sure myself, but I cannot do nothing.

As I said yesterday, I think I am 'growing up'. You will and have always been the most important centre in my life, but now you are not here, I need another road. The poem 'The road less travelled' keeps coming to my mind. Either I sit and look at signposts for the rest of my life, or I take a road, and see where it leads. Well, there you are darling, nothing to do so I philosophise. Which I do a lot these days.

One of the beautiful things to happen today is, it's raining. The smell of wet earth is just wonderful. 3-4 weeks with no rain and temperatures in the 30's. It's just not British is it.

One of the things I miss is reading the newspaper to you and then we discuss parts together. It's so frustrating not to be able to say 'what do you think of this'?

Sue and Adrian have just left after spending quite a lot of time getting my printer to work. I really don't know how I would have managed without them. I do hope it's not all one sided and that I also am of help to them in whatever way they need.

July 2010

Tuesday 13th July

Remember I talked of signposts the other day? Well, I've actually taken one road, it does point me in the direction I want to go, writing. It is only the 1st step, but it is one I've actually taken.

Today I had an answer, and someone is willing to look at what I've written, to start with, these letters to you.

I feel quite sick. What have I started? Can I stand rejection? How do I get it from my scribble to readable papers? Darling, I'm scared and excited, if only I could have your arms around me and your voice saying 'I've told you for years to write' If it should go any further than being looked at I shall feel that at last I am a real me.

To leave something behind for our children, grandchildren, and great grandchildren to read at some point in their lives about 60 years of yours and my life, would be good. Unusually for me, I don't know what to say, oh, I do wish that you could calm me down.

As I said the other day, I feel that I am developing out of my sorrow, and these letters have been my salvation. You have still been there for me, just a little to far away to reach, oh, darling, I'm so excited.

Yes, I'm realistic, I can just hear you saying 'don't count your chickens' and really I'm not, but for me to be recognised as an entity without you is so strengthening.

Maybe tonight I'll sleep without dreams. Love you lots and lots.

July 2010

14th July

And I've just made a mistake. I Went out today to find a photo frame for you, want a picture on my desk. Chose a lovely one, it's black with silver edging. Unfortunately, it looks like I've gone all Victorian and have you in a mourning frame. Oh dear, but it matches the picture of you.

Tonight I didn't want to go out, but was booked to see a flamenco show. Carrie and I had tickets and it was surprisingly good. Guitar just like Julian played and a flamenco dancer.

Songs and dances from different parts of Spain and they were explaining the influence the Arabs had on all their life, but certainly the music. Both the player and the dancer were very good. As so often happens, not enough microphones, or not in the right places, I missed quite a bit of explanation.

This was the last of the Buckingham festival. First time they've done this. Various music every day for a week. I hope that it will be available again next year.

You'd be pleased to see me enjoying life. I certainly do get out more and I feel able to participate more.

July 18

I shouldn't have written that last sentence. I've spent the day being very close to tears. Partly that I'm going through a bad patch vis-a-vis sleeping – or not, would be a better way of putting it. Sleep deprivation when I was nursing you was at least worthwhile, I helped you. This is just sleeplessness. Actually, it makes me quite angry.

July 2010

Adrian has just rung and told me about some research he's found on education, styles of teaching, etc., and we, you and I were at opposite ends of this research. When I get a copy and have read it I'll talk to you about it. Very, very interesting, if only we could talk, you'd be so interested.

Death takes so much away from us, not just your body.

Dr Liz came last night and stayed on her way home. She's looking good and seems to be happy, needs lots of love and gives lots too.

She told me to be kind to myself. Does that mean I can buy a GOOD box of chocolates? No, what I'd really like is for you to be good to me.

How do people survive without love? Even just the memory of it?

That Beatles song 'All You Need Is Love'. So true, so big and so many people needing it? What can one do? Remember what we used to sing at Sunday School? 'You in your small corner, and I in mine'. Really, that is all that as individuals we can do.

The expression I have heard recently is 'hug a hoodie', probably find a load of these trouble-makers just need long term loving. Now I'd be called a 'do-gooder' for saying that.

I suppose our 3 boys had what would be called 'tough love'. A wallop when necessary, but always loved.

You would so enjoy your great granddaughter now. She starts school in September and is very bright and a lot of fun. She and I have a small gnome which we take it in turns to hide in the

garden. She – the gnome – is called Matilda and
she gets put in funny places, but the garden is
small and I'm trying to think where to hide her
next. Sara is a good mum, firm but loving.

Well darling, its nearly 10:pm I will 'awa to ma
bed'. Apart from piles of books, it's empty and I
miss you so much. Love you.

20th July, 4:30am
So far tonight I've had 1 hours sleep. I feel
awful, itching all over. It would seem an easy thing
to diagnose and treat but after all these years still
no answer. As we have said before, man on the
moon but no answer to relatively simple problems.
And of course the money used could be put into
research for diseases like Parkinson's, being
completely selfish, that might have helped you and
many like you. What exactly has been usefully
learnt (that actually is really of use?) by landing
men on the moon? Well, you can tell, can't you,
that I'm tired.

Facing me on this desk is this lovely photo of
you with your big smile. People often say they
loved your smile and dry wit.

At this point I went back to bed again, and still
couldn't sleep!

Today, it is now real morning, 6am, will be hard,
as my head feels as if it's got something inside
squeezing it, sometime today I will probably just
fall asleep.

When I got up again just now I decided to read
something that Adrian had put on my desktop for
me. C.S. Lewis's A Grief Observed. I'm not sure if
you ever read it darling, but now that I too have

had a love, a lover, removed, I can understand what he is saying. Oh to have his knowledge and ability to write like that, his turning away from, then back to, God is just how I felt, and he also found the word DEAD so difficult to understand. I will read it again (not halfway through the night) and I wish I could have met him, and though I have read other books of his, this was the real man.

It's now nearly 7am and I'm going back to bed. I loved and love you and as C.S. Lewis found, loving God becomes a deeper experience. Goodnight, good morning.

22 July

Things are just jumping into my head today, situations before you died, that I wish I'd done differently, regret, such a useless thought to have, unless one learns to pay more attention in future, my future, not yours.

One thing is happening now is that I do think about it in terms of my future. I most certainly want to live before I die, but, what am I trying to work out is, how do I 'go out' and find life.

Sitting here is not good. Life, so I think, is 'out there' and I need to actually look for it, really I think the modern idea is networking. Well, we'll see how my life does grow. If you could I know that you would encourage me. Trouble is, what do I want to do? and what am I capable of doing? Listen to the next thrilling instalment of 'Liz's Life'. Even if I saw a signpost I'm not sure I'd choose the right one.

July 2010

You know how much I loved you and relied on you, its not something we ever talked about was it. Shame, but you always told me to write. Love you.

July 2010

Friday 23rd July

Earlier this year I thought that I would be writing to you less, but it seems that this month has produced more need, not less. If you were just abroad with your work you'd really like my letters, but in this instance, they help me.

The weather thankfully has got cooler and that is a real blessing. We northerners really can't take constant Mediterranean heat, our skin and eyes just aren't right for CONSTANT heat and sun.

However, today I've tidied the garden and it does look good, all swept and watered. Because of the intense heat the garden centres are selling plants off cheap and I have bought 2 pots of the beautiful white lilies I like and that you used to buy me, two for £6, that's cheaper than I can buy the flowers cut, and I have the bulbs for the next few years. So although everything is green in the garden, white lilies are allowed.

It would be wonderful if we could sit out there together, you would like the calmness of the space. Do love you, do miss you, but the world is getting a bit bigger now, don't worry about me. I came from good peasant stock! I will manage.

[No Date]

Reading so much now I can sit in a really comfortable chair, my body is more relaxed. I know you had a recliner chair, but this one is beautifully padded. I've just been reading about separating oneself from the world, as in monasteries, or working from inside the Word. This is a subject I'd love to chew over with you.

July 2010

Very few monks and nuns as we remember them. They, like the rest of us have to change to a large extent, otherwise they are neither feeding themselves or those that need their help. To a greater or lesser degree, everything has to change with changing times. Do you think you would have gone into an order?

I know I couldn't. Now why? Partly I think, because I like the freedom to do what I think is right, that would cause problems of subservience / obedience. It would probably do me good though to be led rather than lead.

The book is called The World Is Our Cloister. We went to hear the author speak and her discussion on the book. A strong woman, both mentally and religiously. Appears to have found her own peace, more so while writing her book.

July 27

These letters will eventually be read by the family so I must be sure that they can understand them. Hence the typing.

These last few days have been full of an awful sadness, deep, deep sadness as if there is no life in me. I am so tired both mentally and physically.

So all sorts of tests will be done, I'm happy about that, but also frightened at what they might find. What is the reason for all this tiredness? If only I could sleep, and sleep but to wake and feel refreshed. There is a part of me that would like to be sleeping by Keith, yet I wouldn't know anything about it. I'm just so full of tears.

Yes, I have lost half my life by Keith's death, and I lost my childhood as well, so there is the future and only I can deal with that, so, Lethbridge, just stop moaning and get on with it. If only you could hold me and say 'it will be alright'. I know that the immediate past is 'alright' but how to alright the future.   I think I'll just go to bed, goodnight darling.

30th July.
Today the heat is so intense that just thinking of the really harsh winter seems to be a good idea. Really I don't remember this sort of intense heat when we were in Africa.

3rd August

Some days you seem very real and close to me-other days I talk to you in my head but I can't write. The last few days have been so full and mixed up and I'm so tired. You could almost go on holiday with the bags under my eyes!

Last Friday I had a consultation with a homeopath and she had a fantastic machine which is called a Bio Resonance something or other. Created by a German and marketed by the Americans. Quite a good combination. One with engineering skills, the other with money.

She is my sort of person, well qualified and enthusiastic. I told her that I chose her because she is German (the home of homeopathy) and her qualifications are good.

Anyway, she, her name is Ute, is starting me on a course of tissue salts, to give me back some energy and also some sleep... . What a wonderful idea!

Yesterday Adrian and Sue came and we moved furniture around ready for today. The new furniture arrives. I think you would like it, a chair and small sofa. Being 5 foot 2, it is just big enough for me to lie down for an afternoon nap. I used to do that so I was near you if you needed me and it was so comfortable, even if the old sofa was the wrong shape. But horror of horrors it cost nearly as much as our first house.

Today we got on to the topic of our role or roles in life at different stages. My thought was that at 78 and a widow I now had no role (especially because of the word 'widow'). Adrian said that I do still have a role, I am still a Mother, that made me think quite a lot about dereliction of duty etc. Asked if I could still give him a thump if necessary: 'Yes if you can catch me'. I am also now known as 'The Matriarch'.

Could I please go back to being your wife and lover? I'm not really greedy, we had a lot of years together, but I am hungry for love, I need you and when I look at your photo and write to you, you are still around. Not morbidly so, but this is my way of managing this great separation.

I suppose at some point I will cease to write to you, but not yet. My need is too great and this is the only way I can be connected to you.

Saturday 7th August.

Just come in from an hour's worth of running to and fro from water butt to plants, and guess what? It's raining. Well I suppose it's good exercise. Spent time this morning looking on the laptop for the poem 'Here' by R.S. Thomas, couldn't find it so, went to our own bookcase, yes, it was there and yes, it's certainly how I feel. 'Sitting at the top of a tree and seeing footsteps that led me here', but the steps only start from when I met you. No footsteps before, just suddenly footsteps x2, yours and mine, thanks darling.

This week I feel as if I've had 2 electric shocks. Suddenly, out of the blue, zing, and a childhood memory came to me. I don't want this at all. After 60 odd years of no memory, I didn't want it now. Didn't want other footsteps going the other way, backwards.

Perhaps it's because I've thought so much recently about writing in general, and one, I imagine, needs a base from which to start to write, but not now.

Must be getting older/wiser. *The Times* now irritates me. So much fashion, sport, or inane chit chat. The only good thing about it, is Libby Purves. I do so like her 'up front' writing. It calls a spade a bloody shovel. No poncing around. But I've had to leave her because the rest of the paper drives me mad.

Today was my first weekend Independent, so much to read, much better. (Also if I don't buy 5 days of *The Times*, and the *Radio Times* (never anything to watch anyway) and just buy one weekend Independent I save about £22 a month). Don't laugh at me darling, I am getting better at sums.

It was always so easy to just say 'Keith what's ...' and get an immediate answer. You were good at so many things.

What a day. I sometimes think how much easier it would have been to have you cremated. No, I don't like cremation and I wanted to have somewhere to go to touch base, but the grave's causing lots of problems.

We went to put the stone on the grave today and it is too small. Nothing is in proportion and I want it to be nice, but we've had to be so careful of the money. And as I've said to Adrian, I've never done a grave before, I'm an interior designer, not a grave designer. We have been all over the place trying to find a base for the plaques and can't find what we want.

The plaque is too square for an oblong grave. Oh, dear darling, dying was the easy part, but getting it fixed now is hard, and very costly.

I really thought that today would be a final act of settling you, but no.

August 17th

It seems ages since I last wrote to you. Actually a mixture of living through a period of desperate tiredness with splitting headaches. I've been going to bed at 7-8 just to get my clothes off and to lie flat.

Another reason is that in spite of wanting to be with you or you with me, I am managing my life in a much better way now. Feels almost like being more grown up and taking control of my own life. You would I think be pleased about that.

Putting the experience of death, and dying, and grief to some positive use, I'm thinking of being a representative on a board dealing with various end of life issues at the local hospital.

We were very fortunate that I could nurse you at home with the help of the hospice nurses. This is why I feel that I can use both yours and my experiences to help others.

I think you would approve, thus, nothing about you and the finality of death has been wasted. Your brain (by your choice) went to research into Parkinson's disease, and now, the actual experience of death and dying is being put to use. Looking back over our life I don't think we wasted it. When we were younger I wish that we had done more walking, climbing etc., but we did have a lot of fun anyway and enjoyed our life, each other, and our sons. Goodnight darling

August 18th

The book I'm reading now so reminds me of you and your unknown Jewishness. Roots and Shoots by Harold Jacobson. It is an interesting book on so many levels. There is philosophy, history, language, geography et al. And over all of this the wonderful interplay of people, and in this case so many different nations as he tries to find his roots. In this story he finds the reason for so many things that he just is and does. Just like you.

I do so wish that you and I could have gone this road of discovery together. So many things that we have joked over and wondered at. The deep feeling that you always had that somehow it was right for you to pay homage at one of the concentration camps. All of this was not nurture but nature, a nature unknown. This also explains your deep spiritual life.

Although this life of yours, the Jewishness is not passed down through my line, as I am not Jewish, your life style (and the looks) most certainly are. All good things to pass on to our sons, and by descent, our grandchildren etc.

Anyway I wish you could have read it, or I read it to you. There's so much there that we would have enjoyed chatting over. That is what loss is, No one to bounce thoughts off.

My man my loss. Now I must be practical, go and do some work. Goodnight darling.

August 19th.

Today I've been wrapping care parcels. Julian and Stefanie can't get Bird's custard powder in Germany, please would I send them one or two? They do like to have a proper apple pie and custard. Julian was saying the other day how suddenly he turns round and expects you to be there next to him. All the boys miss you in different ways, but miss you still the same.

Stefanie sent me some money as a present for myself so, this week I am going to have some reflexology, it really makes me feel good.

Within the next few weeks I have so many tests to be done to find out what makes me tick … or doesn't as the case maybe.

Maybe I shall become the 5 foot 2, 8 stone girl you fell in love with!

Remember the boys looking at a picture of you and I at 19? Well I can see what Dad saw in you Mum, but what did you see in him? You were gawky at that age and only a little heavier than me. It was definitely the potential ...

A book I picked up for £1 this week by Rabbi Julia Neuberger. I'm not Dead Yet, to do with ageing and that we must not be sidelined. This I agree with, but if only we can learn from youth and they can learn from age ... But 'twas ever thus.

Ah, one more thing, Carrie, Rosemary and I have been invited to a retirement party on Saturday night. I am going to dress 'posh' for a change. Love you.

20th August.

Just had a phone call from Carrie.

Would I like to go to an auction? Silly question, I think the last one we went to was in Wales and I bought those 3 investiture chairs which I then sold to pay for our holiday. That was the time that you kept nudging me to stop, only I thought you meant to carry on. Still we had a good holiday. Second hand Rose again.

This auction was really a glorified boot sale, so no money made this time.

Do you sense that I'm growing up? Not growing away from you, that would never happen, but just learning to plough my own furrow. Lovely expression that. We do have a very rich language don't we. A very old saying but still having meaning today.

Sat. 21 Aug.

How do I explain today?

It was meant to be a lie in.

7.10 am Wake up and go to bathroom.

9.00am. No paper delivered, go and get it (necessary to put clothes on). I wanted a slummocking day. No not to be

11.30am. Adrian and Sue arrive for pre-arranged lunch. Good, all goes well, lovely chat.

2.00pm. Must check bank, going out tomorrow.

2.10. Have just managed to lock my bank account!

2.15. Rang bank, some stripling youth from Outer Patagonia tries to talk me through the system. Difficult with deaf old lady.

Gets madam to type in numbers, which I do.

2.30. Tries to talk deaf old lady through system yet again. Adrian in stitches while stripling youth at other end still trying to get me reconnected. Adrian tries to explain to me that when stripling youth says to type in number he does not mean into computer but into telephone!

3.00.pm. All calm. I have now unlocked my bank, good job as I am going to craft fair tomorrow.

3.30-5.00 Try to rest as I am going to a party tonight. 65 + retirement.

Did hair. Dress and tart up. (Actually you would have liked the look of me tonight, I quite liked the look of me myself.)

7.00 pm. 2 friends come and we walk up together. Music heard a mile off.

Find table as far away as possible from band and by 8.00pm eyes crossing with decibel levels. How do the youngsters ever manage to speak to each other?

8.45. Speeches toasts clapping and dancing.

9.00. Our table just about speechless with shouting at each other, plus me deaf in one ear and the man opposite me deaf in both. But being British we of course smiled benignly and carried on partying. Actually is was a good party and there was a lot of dancing. I excused myself by saying the only dance I ever learnt was the jitterbug!

10.00. I slide graciously I hope out of side door, having said thank you to host.

10.30. Home, ah bliss, not a sound. Peace and quiet. I did enjoy myself but at heart I am not a party person. Having said that we have given masses of parties and people always enjoyed them.

One thing you would have liked tonight, being a purveyor of nice hands, mine are nice now. My hands are not in water so much and my nails are growing, in fact I actually had nail polish on, looked good. One of the nice things you said to me before you died was that you always knew it was my hands touching you even if you couldn't see me.

One more thing about today, I've learnt how to text on the mobile. Clever stuff, but I refuse to use text spelling.

22nd Aug.

The craft fair was good. It was at Mentmore House so it was quite upmarket. Lots of very good stuff, woodturning that you would have enjoyed. There was a lot of very fashionable clothes, scarves, shirts etc., and of course lots of food.

The only thing I really bought was a small Isfahan rug to hang on the wall. You know how I love textiles on the walls. It is the really deep red that I like and it just lifts the sitting room walls. You would like it too.

When I came home I set to, and have cleared the kitchen table and set up my painting paraphernalia and I am going to try and paint a picture, probably of a boat or boats, we'll see. As you can see, I'm trying to make life a little larger for myself. I will not mope. I found a book in our bookcase on painting with acrylics that I had bought for you when you couldn't do fine watercolours anymore, so that is what I'm going to do.

Really I'm quite excited, I love doing something new, but, I don't think I'll be as good as you. You really had so many talents that we were going to utilise on retirement. But that was not to be.

So I will have my reading writing painting and gardening and music, this hopefully will give me a pattern for living.

When you died obviously a part, a large part of me also died. But I have had to find another me. As I have said before 17-77, I have been two halves all those years, now I am just one half swimming in a great big sea and I'm not a good swimmer, but I keep on paddling ...

Now I think I am able to function on a certain level. Not with putting people or pursuits where you used to be but finding facets of myself that perhaps didn't work as a twosome but function better as a single being. Which of course is what we are. We are born alone we die alone and if in the interim we reach our own zenith then we are very blessed.

All this probably means I won't write to you so often as I will have developed some strengths of my own. You are still my man and I love you so much. Soon I will write maybe a story of your/our life. I'd like to write a column for a paper or magazine, something short and sweet (but not sticky).

Change is not always a bad thing is it?

When C.S. Lewis write about his wife's death, he wrote four diaries and said that is enough I must go forward. I read *A Grief Observed* and wish I had that man's reasoning powers and his knowledge, but our pain is the same and we all come through this in our own way.

As I seem to be in a philosophical mood, a quote I like from Shakespeare, 'We are such stuff as dreams are made on, and our little life is rounded with a sleep.'

Goodnight darling sleep well.

Sunday 5th October 2010

This is nearly the end of my 5th large diary of letters to you darling, and I think this will be the last real letter I write to you.

Not that I have no love/longing or care for you but I have grown up. The loss is still there, but not so much of the need I've had to always be with you in spirit. I have taken on more of life and living. I've put them into places I used to share with you, and now, just to myself because I have to. Twenty months ago you died, became dead, left, I became widowed, got left behind, all these emotions, I've tried to channel into a different life.

I think I'm sort of succeeding and as I say, growing up. I don't have to like it, but I have to do it.

The very first meeting that I am now part of 'End of Life Care' seems to be something I can get my teeth into. Just a group of us (about 8) with Head of End of Life Care as the 'boss-woman' looking for help from us, the public, to help get the white paper really looked at and worked through.

You would actually have enjoyed doing it yourself, very professionally, but I like to think you'd want me to be part of this now. It will entail meeting with different sections of the public, so my knowledge will increase.

This last week has been very hard on me. I had my other eye done under general this time because I was terrified of the pain. Fine, I didn't feel it, not till I came round and boy it hurt then. Do wish I knew why. It makes me feel quite ill.

I have a sort of vertigo and wobble all over the place; glad I haven't got 3 eyes! Not much work done this week, mustn't bend, mustn't lift, dizzy, etc. Boring.

Anyway, today we went to your grave to put the slab down. A large heather-slate slab from Wales, with a granite slab on top, looks good. We have almost finished your grave; it's still settling and will need some more chippings down. Do that when Gordon comes.

Stood looking at the grave today and found it very hard to think of YOU there. It has become just a place now. One that I will keep nice, just because I've always kept you nice, but you, my Keith, you are now in the photo on my desk, in objects round the flat, in my thoughts and ideas, much more real here now. You share my thoughts in my head; it's a closer way of being together. Always around, not so much on my own now.

This I am sure must be the norm of grieving, the stages you go through and then almost you're together again. For now my darling, this will be my last letter, full of my love and longing and my tears, but I have come through and for now I need to stop. There will be times when I will have to write again, but for now, sleep well my darling, always yours, Liz.

Two Poems by Keith

Two Poems by Keith

You Are the Wind Under My Wings

Another day, another journey.
Today shall I fly, free high and happy?
This day shall I touch the untouchable

And soar on wings of love and peace?
Or this day into the reality of life
Here on earth shall I fall?

How hard to soar above war, strife,
Hunger, the anger of man to man.
How much we long for 'the wings of
A dove' to fly away.

But for a short time here our wings are clipped.
Yet one day – one day, I will feel
Your breath of wind under my wings
And I will fly high, so high.

I am a Leaf in Autumn

I am frightened.
I am clinging on like grim death to my big master
tree.
It is a long way down to the bottom,
And I do not,
I definitely do not,
Want to let go.
Most of my mates have gone
And they look as if they have landed safely.
But that does not make it any easier
For me to let go.

But I will have to very soon,

Two Poems by Keith

I can feel my toes getting weaker,
And my fingers too.
Oh dear, here we go.
No.
My eyes are shut tight,
I have to let go.
Now.
I must let go.
I am scared.

Here we go.
I have to let go
And I am floating downwards.
Still floating.

Plop.
Right on top of my mates.
Gently,
Nothing to be afraid of.
I made it.
But oh! I was scared.

Hello Everybody.

Printed in Great Britain
by Amazon